THE ENDLESS WAVE

Skateboarding, Death & Spirituality

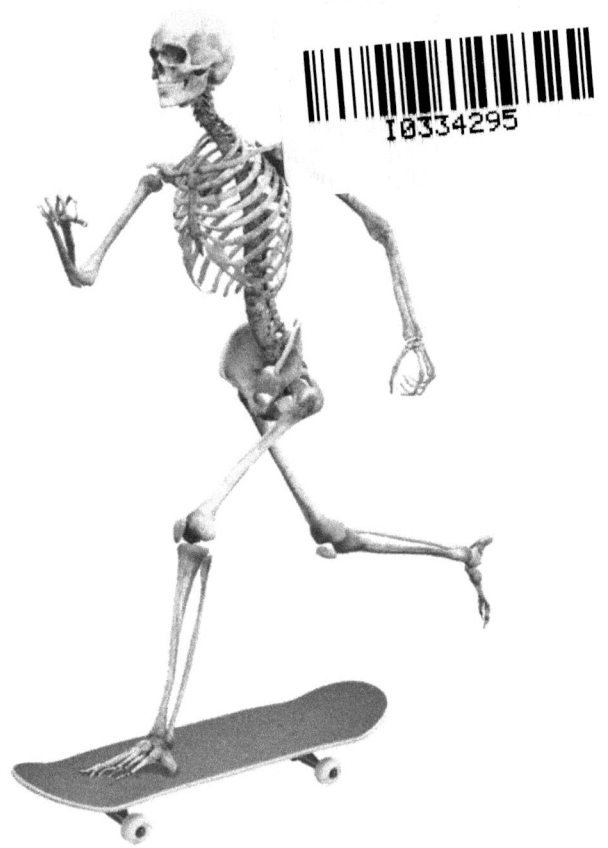

MICHAEL BROOKE & NATHAN HO

Copyright © 2023 by Michael Brooke & Nathan Ho
All rights reserved. No portion of this book may be reproduced—mechanically, electronically, or by any other means, including photocopying—without written permission of the publisher.
All personal vignettes and anecdotes are from the author's lives or sources referenced.

Printed in Australia

THE ENDLESS WAVE
Skateboarding, Death & Spirituality

*This book is dedicated
to all skaters past, present and future.*

PUBLISHED BY
MICHAEL BROOKE & NATHAN HO

IN COLLABORATION WITH

TABLE OF CONTENT

PART ONE
A Skategeezer Ruminates on Death & Dying 1

Balancing the Risk vs. Reward 5
Reality Doesn't Just Bite, It Spits! 7
Inner Strength 11
In Memoriam 15
Suicide, Skaters and Me 21
Sudden Death 27
Life and Rebirth 31
Best Made Plans 35
A Wall of Resources 37
From Woo Woo To Wow 39
Things Said And Not Said 43
The Real Bucket List 45
While You Can Still Push 49
The Magic Of Balance 51
The List 55
Difficult People & Death 57
Regret 61
The Who What, Where, When, Why and How of Death 65
A Celebration of Life 69
A Planned Death 73
Grief 75
Some Final Thoughts 79
Postscript (The Future Is Unwritten) 83

TABLE OF CONTENT

PART TWO
Taking Things to a Whole Other Level 85

Inspiration For The Endless Wave 87

Freeing Skateboarders from the Fear of Death 91

Skateboarding and the Language of Love..99

Different Styles, Different Smiles 101

Skateboarding and The Soul 105

"The Key to Immortality is to Live a Life Worth Living"..................109

The Halfpipe of Grief...115

The Third-Eye of Skateboarders 121

Skateboarders and Suicide 125

Skating for Passion and Purpose 131

Skateboarders, Cause, Effect and Responsibility 135

Skateboarders and Sacred Space 141

Skateboarders and Compassion 145

Skateboarding as Prayer and Meditation 149

Skateboarding and Spiritual Maintenance 155

Skateboarding: Empowerment, Enrichment & Enlightenment 161

Afterword by Nathan 167

PART ONE

A Skategeezer Ruminates on Death & Dying

Introduction By Michael Brooke

Millions of articles, books, videos, podcasts and pieces of art are dedicated to the ideas surrounding death and dying. But I'd wager a large fortune that very few of them give a perspective of death and dying through the lens of a skateboarder. This book aims to do just that — or at least start a conversation or two.

Firstly, I am not an expert in skateboarding, but I enjoy it immensely. I've been joyfully riding since 1975 and pride myself on riding all types of terrain with all types of boards. I enjoy street, vert, transition, longboarding, and freestyle and I'll even run slalom cones. My journey writing about skateboarding started in 1995 with this article: *www.dansworld.com/michael.html*

Dansworld was one of the first websites on skateboarding and I was fortunate to be able to write about my experiences. Full disclosure: I got the date wrong (I started riding in 1975, not 1976), but everything else is spot on. The site inspired me to create my own website. I called it The SkateGeezer Homepage. It aimed to publicize older skateboarders and get them thinking about the nostalgic side of riding. Visit the page, if you dare, but I warn you, the graphics are pretty brutal. Then again what do you expect, it was created over 25 years ago! *www.interlog.com/~mbrooke/skategeezer.html*

The SkateGeezer Homepage led to a book contract and in 1999, *The Concrete Wave* (the history of skateboarding) was published. It sold 42,000 copies and launched a 52-part TV series. After this, I launched *International Longboarder Magazine* in the summer of 1999. This magazine eventually became *Concrete Wave* and I published and edited it until the summer of 2018. Here's a collection of issues: *issuu.com/concretewaves*

When I decided to sell the magazine, it was because I felt that it was time to do something else. Initially, I thought I'd move into working at a non-profit. It turned out that my life was going to go in a different direction. I wound up answering a job advertisement at a local funeral home. I had done some volunteer work at a nearby hospice and retirement home. After my interview, they asked me to come in for a day to try things. This was late June of 2018, and something about the job felt right.

So, for the last five years or so, I've been working as a funeral director's assistant. It was quite a transition from publishing. I pretty much do everything but arrange funerals. From premature babies to those over 100 years old, I've experienced death up close and personal. I've done dozens of house calls to transfer the deceased back to our funeral home and assisted at well over 700 funerals.

It's been over three years since I wrote about skateboarding and over 25 years since I connected with Dansworld to write my first piece. It feels wonderful to be writing again.

I want to thank my family, My wife Michal, daughter Maya and sons Jonathan and Ethan. They have been incredibly supportive of everything I've done. They've also been monumentally patient and understanding too. Without them, I'd be nowhere. I'd also like to thank Nathan Ho for inspiring me and being a catalyst for me to start writing again.

I hope that this book inspires my fellow skateboarders to think about death and dying from a different perspective — a perspective that is uniquely ours. Thank you for taking the time to read it.

Note: I left the funeral home at the end of April, 2023. I now dedicate my time to capturing and preserving memories, writing and inspiring others to find their passion, purpose and meaning.

I will never stop skateboarding.

Balancing the Risk vs Reward

Think about the first time you stepped on a board. Were you a little bit scared or anxious? Chances are you might have had some trepidation, but it was mitigated by the sheer joy and freedom you saw other skaters experiencing and you wanted some of that! So, you took a chance, jumped on the board and were hopefully rewarded.

It is not just a question of balancing on a skateboard, but how you balance the risk vs the reward. Skateboarders know that falling can produce painful and sometimes lethal consequences. But all those worries and fears are cast aside for the reward that is riding.

Now think about the first time you learned to drop in on a mini-ramp or bowl. Again, you probably felt a little anxious but knew instinctively that the reward would be truly worthwhile. It is the combination of risk vs reward that forms the first part of a skater's lens and we carry this throughout our life.

What I have learned in my 59+ years of living and 48+ years of riding a skateboard, is that sometimes, you have to jump right in, despite the difficulty or risk. Built into the DNA of skateboarding is risk and I know for a fact that it has changed the way I look at death and dying. While it can be risky to skateboard, I feel that the greater risk is not living a fulfilling, joyful life.

The countless hours spent with friends skateboarding create a unique bond. Sure, there are times you are competing in a game of skate or who can go the fastest down a hill, but mostly the ride is the reward. Think of the road trips you've been on with your fellow skaters. That first push can lead to a lifetime of freedom and exploration. For me, skateboarding was a catalyst to lead me to people, music, art and ideas that I normally wouldn't have discovered. The more you commit, the greater the reward.

Skateboarders know all about quality time — especially if you're living in a climate that is not sunny all the time. We cherish the opportunity to ride with friends. But most importantly, we value the time put into riding a skateboard. We know that at any moment, a pebble, car or crack in the pavement could stop us in our tracks.

When I attend a funeral, I can tell almost immediately what kind of eulogies I will hear. If the family is tight-knit and supportive of one another, the eulogies will often be about the time the person put into people. While hearing about a person's business or academic accomplishments can be impressive, it is the anecdotes about the time spent with family and friends that really leave an impression on me. I have never once heard "I wish my father would have spent less time with us" or "I wish my mom would have spent more time at the office."

Ultimately, life is about balance. If you are obsessed with skateboarding to the point that it leaves you penniless, you've gone too far. Conversely, there are so many millions of people afraid to take that first push or to "drop in." They firmly believe that life is scary and meant to be cautiously navigated. Their fears can lead to frustration, anger and depression. It makes for a joyless life. Skateboarding has a magical way of creating a sense of freedom in your mind. Once your mind is free, anything is possible. After all, you have a 100% chance of dying. The question is what are you going to do about it?

Reality Doesn't Just Bite, It Spits!

Before I start this next chapter, I wanted to preface things with a small warning. The truth is that discussing death and dying can be very difficult for some. Nathan and I are going to hit on some very challenging and somewhat painful ideas over the course of this book. But if you picked up on what I was writing about in Chapter One, I think you'll do just fine.

The following incident happened about five years ago, but I remember it like it was yesterday. I had been at my job as a funeral director's assistant for less than a week. It was a blazing hot day in July and I was getting to know my fellow co-workers. At the cemetery, we had spied someone lurking about 200 feet away. We were told that it was an estranged brother who was not invited to the funeral, but had somehow found out the time and place and was making his presence known. It created a little bit of intrigue, but none of us were concerned that he would do something to disrupt the funeral.

As this was literally my second or third time attending a funeral at a gravesite, I wasn't really sure if having a lurker was a normal occurrence or something completely uncommon. It turned out to be something else — it turned out to be completely off the rails. The funeral service took about 30 minutes to finish. The family left the grave and slowly the brother walked up to the grave. He stood in front of the grave and spat on it. Then he said, "I'm glad you're dead, you f--g c--t." He promptly left and I stood there with my jaw dropped. As he left, I could feel the tension and anger just swirling around him. I was literally stunned into silence.

I am happy to report that a scene like this is NOT a common occurrence. The amount of visceral hatred that seethed in this man's veins was both intense and shocking. While I will never know what led up to this moment, it is forever seared in my brain. A fellow staff member remarked that he'd been working in funeral services for over 25 years and had never encountered something like this before. I guess in some crazy way, my timing was pretty good.

There is no doubt in my mind that you gain an incredible appreciation for life when you are surrounded by death. It seems oddly counter-intuitive and yet I encounter it constantly. What can we learn from my story about this man? I think you could spend many years trying to unpack a scene like this, but I think it boils down to just one crucial thing. *"You gotta handle your shit, or shit will handle you."*

Clearly, this man (who appeared to be in his mid 60's) and his mother (along with the rest of the family) needed help. He clearly carries a burning resentment that was overwhelming. Whatever the history is between the family, it would appear that it was never dealt with. This man needed help. Maybe he got it, but I sense it never really helped sufficiently. Or maybe, in the last three years, he did receive some help. I can only hope that he did. Sadly, I will never know.

Skaters come from a variety of backgrounds. Some are rich, some are poor and some are middle class. I would venture a guess that a number of skaters turned to skateboarding because it was a path to freedom from an issue. These issues or problems can range from mild to severe. No matter what a skater tries to leave behind (ie: an abusive home, inattentive parents, abusive sibling or some other problem) the fact remains that skateboarding can't fully erase the problem. Coming to terms with this can be both alarming and painful but it is necessary.

Make no mistake, I am glad I had skateboarding when I was younger. It wasn't just a creative outlet, it provided me with a great deal of support. But in truth,

I never dealt with certain shit until I reached my 50s. Of course, things change with time and nowadays, people are a lot more open to dealing with mental health issues. But the reality is that if you use skateboarding as your only path to freedom, you aren't dealing with the problem. This can have a substantially negative impact as you move through life.

If you carry with you hatred against people who don't look like you or skate like you, it is you who have the problem. Skateboarding promotes freedom, but if you are running away from an issue that needs to be dealt with, you will never be truly free.

This is a hard truth but it is critical to accept. As much as we love skateboarding or any other activity, it can't truly replace family or close friends. A skateboarder knows instinctively to value each moment riding — whether alone or in a group. But as you move from adolescence to middle age and beyond, you realize that skeletons in closets have a peculiar way of rearing their heads. Whatever demons you may carry, skateboarding has proven to be a great way to keep them at bay. But the demons won't fully be exercised until you face reality.

I have tried yoga, cooking, gardening and conversing in another language. At some point or another, these activities have let me down, often with ridiculous and embarrassing results. I used to say that skateboarding never let me down. But the fact is that skateboarding is an activity, not a person. No matter how much you love your skateboard or the act of skateboarding, it will never love you back. It can't because a skateboard is an inanimate object. An object that certainly improves your life, but it is only an object.

Skateboarding will be the catalyst for you to have experiences that you will love. It will often bring you people you might grow to cherish (and respect). But the fact remains your skateboard will outlive you. In a hundred years from now, your descendants might know that you skated. But one thing is for certain. If you don't handle your shit eventually, your descendants will have to.

Inner Strength

Some of you might be wondering what exactly is my job as a funeral director's assistant. The best way to answer this is to say I do many different things, but I don't make the actual arrangements for the funeral service. I am there to help out during a funeral to make sure things run smoothly. All the arrangements with the clergy, cemetery, family etc are handled by other people. I also assist at the chapel and cemetery with the service.

Perhaps the most unique part of my job is the interaction I have with families when a death has occurred in a home, hospice or hospital. This is something that very few people have an opportunity to witness and that includes most of the funeral directors or managers at my funeral home. So, what I am about to share with you is insider information.

When we get a call that someone has died, we are usually sent in a team of two. We call this a transfer. It is a polite way of saying that we're picking up a dead person. It is indeed a heavy feeling approaching someone's door and knocking. They have dreaded this moment. But we approach with a solemn attitude and carefully assess the situation.

We mostly transfer people who are old. They can be in their late 70's, 80's or 90's. Very rarely do we transfer someone who has lived past 100. Thankfully, it is also very rare that we transfer someone who is young. I will discuss what it is like dealing with young people in a future chapter.

As we move the body from the bed to the stretcher, we are careful to ensure the body is treated with the utmost respect. All eyes are on us. Sometimes, the family won't want to be present as we move the body from the bed to the stretcher. Other times, they will glare at us with an intensity that is almost palpable. They are watching our every move. I don't blame them — after all, we are doing something that they hoped would never happen. We can't make any mistakes. Sometimes a body will be fairly light. Other times, we encounter quite a bit of difficulty in moving someone. We have to be very careful that we don't hit any walls or fall with the stretcher down the stairs.

Many times, if a person has died at home, you will encounter the caregivers along with the family members. While the caregivers are not related by blood to the deceased, they grieve just as much. Sometimes, they grieve even more.

Entering someone's private home who you don't know can be somewhat surreal. You're not there to pay a social visit. It's not an open house or a party. You have to be very aware of your surroundings. Respect is the keyword along with keeping a level head. You must remain professional and calm, even though you are witnessing death up close. It's not a movie or reality tv — it is just reality.

I'd say that to do this type of work, you need a fair amount of emotional intelligence. What is emotional intelligence? Here's a definition I found:

Emotional intelligence (or emotional quotient or EQ) is the ability to understand, use, and manage your emotions positively to relieve stress, communicate effectively, empathize with others, overcome challenges and defuse conflict.

Believe it or not, I think EQ is something that some skateboarders have a genuine gift for. You need the ability to read a situation quickly. Death brings about so many emotions. Empathy plays a big role. There is grief, relief and in some cases genuine surprise. I once picked up a 98-year-old and the spouse was crying and wailing. She couldn't believe her husband had died. She was in shock. I thought to myself "the guy was 98, how can she be surprised?" But I knew well enough to keep my thoughts to myself.

As a skateboarder, I am sure there have been times when your ability to read a situation quickly paid off immeasurably. It might have been those times when you questioned authority. Perhaps a security guard (or irate neighbor) chased you away from a great spot. I am sure you've experienced a motorist loudly honking their horn at you as you effortlessly ride down the road. Skateboarders, in many cases, are doing something that can be considered "quasi" legal. Your ability to keep cool with authority is an excellent skill.

If you're not getting badgered by authority figures, you might find that you're encountering people who show absolute disdain for your chosen pastime. I've encountered numerous individuals who seem to question why on earth I'd even skateboard at "my age." I always laugh when people say I'm too old to be riding a skateboard. Their incorrect perception won't dampen my joy one bit. But I never lose my temper with them.

The truth is that while most of our time as skaters is pretty stress-free, there are also times when things can get out of hand. I've been in a few hairy situations which have required a very calm and collected mindset. It's not so much what you're experiencing, but how you are handling it.

Your willingness to continue to skate despite all these obstacles showcases a unique type of resiliency. It is a resilience that can be drawn upon as you deal with other types of precarious situations.

This ability to adapt, manage stress and overcome challenges is a critical part of being a skater. But I'd go one step further. If you're brave enough to charge downhill at 50 mph or drop into a 15-foot high half-pipe, then I think it can be excellent mental preparation for the challenges of death and dying.

Emotional intelligence plays a huge role in dealing with death and dying. If you draw on your experiences as a skater, you will find an inner strength you might not know you had.

In Memoriam

One of the most amazing things about skateboarding is that its superstars tend to be within reach of the ordinary skater. For example, Tony Alva can be found hanging out at numerous events. There are dozens of skateparks that are frequented by pros worldwide. Even at a contest, many pro skaters are accessible. If you are fortunate enough to attend the Skateboarding Hall of Fame (in California) as a fan, you'll have an opportunity to be with many legends.

It is the accessible nature of skateboarding that makes it vastly different from other sports. Since it's not the same size as professional football, basketball or baseball, it remains something that true fans can embrace without destroying their savings account.

Thanks to my role as a writer and publisher within the skate industry, I've had many opportunities to meet some of the movers and shakers. While death takes out many professional athletes, it would appear that skateboarding seems to suffer more than its fair share of losses. Many are under 60.

I went through this list and started to pick out skaters who I had either met or spent some time with. It was quite an overwhelming feeling. So, for my own sanity (and probably yours as well) I am going to break this up over a series of chapters. It will be in chronological order and I hope it gives you some insight to the vast number of truly remarkable people I've had the privilege of knowing.

I am going to start with Tim Brauch. Tim was someone I met at the Action Sports Retailer show. He died in May 1999, and I think I met him in January of that year. He would have been 24 at the time. My most vivid memory was just how incredibly friendly and down-to-earth he was. He seemed to possess very little ego. How I truly wish I'd been able to spend more time with him.

Next up is Bobby Turner. Bobby was a legend in the world of slalom back in the 1970s. His boards were extremely expensive back then. I met Bobby briefly and I recall him having a huge amount of skate stoke. The resurgence of slalom skateboarding seemed to be nurturing his soul.

Although not a professional skater, Fausto Vitello left a huge mark on the skateboarding industry. He was the co-founder of many of the brands you know and cherish. He helped establish Thrasher Magazine, Independent Trucks, Thunder and Real — just to name a few. I had the opportunity to speak with Fausto at length when I was doing my research for the book The *Concrete Wave*. He spent over 2 hours with me on the phone and the result was a hefty piece in the book. Oddly enough, the folks from Transworld Skateboarding never returned my calls and were pissed that they didn't receive the same type of coverage that Thrasher had in my book.

Fausto died suddenly riding his bicycle at age 59. What is most intriguing is that the New York Times contacted me about his passing. With respect to the obituary, it appears I seemed to be one of their only sources for the piece. The folks at Thrasher didn't seem interested in returning their calls. This is ironic in so many ways. I am publishing the piece in its entirety so you can understand my point.

Fausto Vitello, an entrepreneur and publisher who helped take the dying pastime of skateboarding out of the suburbs and into the streets, where it became a rude and riotous multibillion-dollar business, died Saturday while riding his bicycle in Woodside, Calif. He was 59 and lived in Hillsborough, Calif.

The apparent cause was a heart attack, his family said.

Mr. Vitello was revered by skateboarders (and reviled by their parents) as a founder and the president of Thrasher magazine, which for a quarter-century has been the rebellious bible of the skateboarding subculture. He was also a founder of Independent Trucks, a leading manufacturer of skateboard equipment, clothing and accessories.

"He's the godfather of punk-rock skateboarding," Michael Brooke, the publisher of Concrete Wave, a skateboarding magazine based in Toronto, said in a telephone interview yesterday.

Published monthly, Thrasher has a circulation of about 175,000. Its Web site, thrashermagazine.com, features articles, interviews and, for school-age readers, a selection of downloadable term papers "to free up more time to skate."

Skateboarding has been around since the early 1900s when some thrill-seeking child first nailed a two-by-four to a roller skate. Conditions improved in the late 1950s when the first commercial skateboards were marketed, and again in the early 70s, when urethane wheels and better boards made fancy maneuvers possible.

By the mid-70s, skateboarding was hugely popular among suburban boys, who performed in empty swimming pools and in specially built skateboard parks. By the end of the decade, however, many towns, concerned about liability, razed their parks, and the sport went into decline.

But it was still possible to skate in the streets, using features of the urban landscape — curbs, steps, railings, benches — as launching pads from which to take flight. Mr. Vitello, a devoted skateboarder who had founded Independent Trucks in 1978, capitalized on the fledgling sport of street skating, starting Thrasher with several associates in 1981.

With its mantra "skate and destroy," the magazine embodied the punk-rock ethos of the day, exhorting readers to devote their lives to their art. And if the pursuit of art happened to involve some imbibing and inhaling, it implied, that was all right, too.

"Thrasher magazine has had its detractors," Mr. Brooke said. "Fausto and Thrasher, had no problem being very — how can I put this? — gnarly. There are swear words; there is a whole violent side to it. There are a lot of parents who forbid their children to read Thrasher."

Fausto Vitello was born in Buenos Aires on Aug. 7, 1946, and came to the United States with his family as a boy. He grew up in the Haight-Ashbury district of San Francisco and earned a bachelor's degree in Spanish from San Francisco State University.

Mr. Vitello is survived by his wife, the former Gwynn Rose, and their children, Tony and Sally, all of Hillsborough; a sister, Lidia, of Elburn, Ill.; and his mother, Aurora, of San Francisco.

Today, skateboarding is a $2 billion industry, according to Mr. Brooke. And as the sport has been embraced by mainstream culture, including ESPN and the X Games, its roughest edges have been smoothed away.

This did not sway Mr. Vitello from his original vision. "Fausto never cleaned up," Mr. Brooke said. "You open up Thrasher and it's still guys drinking and shooting guns."

Next up is Warren Bolster who was both an incredible photographer and editor of SkateBoarder Magazine. I could write at least four chapters about my experiences with Warren. Like Fausto, Warren died in 2006 and he too died at the same age — 59. In fact, they both died within 5 months of each other. Warren's drive to build skateboarding during its second boom in the mid-70s almost took him out.

Unlike most of the people that I am discussing in this article, Warren Bolster wasn't just someone I met briefly or conducted an interview with. I actually worked very closely with him for a period of a year. We worked on a book called The Legacy of Warren Bolster.

When I first met Warren, he was battling his addictions. He was also quite a curmudgeon. He had a temper and he wasn't the easiest guy to work with. At the same time, his patience and trust in me with the book project was something that I'll never forget. Warren left SkateBoarder Magazine in a cloud of controversy. His fondness for a certain illicit drug was his undoing. The publishers were begging him to get treatment. When he was let go, they had to replace him with at least four people. He was a workaholic with a vision to make skateboarding something insanely great. Warren contributed a huge amount to skateboarding and it was a privilege to know him.

Unfortunately, much of Warren's slides had been either stolen or lost in the twenty or so years since he had left the magazine. There were so many photos that I so truly wished we'd had the opportunity to publish, but they had long since disappeared.

Warren's task was to identify each of the slides that I had chosen. I also asked him to write about the skater in the photo and what was happening at the time. Thankfully, with most of the photos, his memory was crystal clear.

The book was actually financed by Kevin Harris, the owner of Ultimate Skateboard Distribution. Although Kevin never recouped his investment, the ripple effect of his patronage was enormous. A number of magazines and books have reprinted these photos. He eventually wound up being inducted into the Skateboarding Hall of Fame.

In 2004, the Legacy of Warren Bolster (Master of Skateboard Photography) was released. I brought Warren to San Diego to be at the launch of the book at the Action Sports Retailer show. The experience remains one of my top 5 moments during my time as a publisher. The ASR show brought together the heavyweights in skateboarding and surfing. We had Warren stationed at a company called Video Action Sports. This was a time before YouTube and people actually bought videotapes and DVDs for their own personal viewing.

As soon as the launch began, I knew we had a very cool experience brewing. People that hadn't seen Warren in over 2 decades came up and shook his hand and hugged him. It was a who's who of the skate and surf industries. There was a feeling that Warren was finally getting his due. I felt proud to be a part of it and I knew Warren felt good.

The show ended and we tried our best to market the book. In hindsight, I should have known it was a recipe for failure. Four thousand copies of the book were printed in Canada. This meant they were expensive to produce. A $40 retail price didn't help the situation. Realistically, there wasn't the demand we initially thought there would be. We should have printed overseas with a run of 1,000. But this was the first book I'd ever published and it was one heck of a learning curve.

Warren was very aggravated by the failure of the book to take off. I felt very badly about things, but as much as I tried, the demand just wasn't there. Nowadays, if you go searching for the book, it is a collectors item. I've seen copies sell for over $500!

The years following the publication of the book were not good for Warren. Although he had received treatment for his drug addiction just after the book launch, it failed to truly improve his life to any great extent. Sadly, he was involved in a car accident which left him with crippling pain and he returned to using painkillers.

Unfortunately, Warren was never able to get a handle on the demons that plagued him for decades. Tragically, he committed suicide in Hawaii in 2006, almost two years to the day that I met him at the book launch in San Diego.

I walked the ASR show with deep sadness but with the knowledge that I'd at least helped keep the memory of Warren Bolster alive.

Learn more about Warren here:

Suicide, Skaters and Me

I just worked at a funeral service that thankfully, we don't see too often. It was for a middle-aged man who was a husband, father, camp director and artist. At age 47, he decided that the depression he was battling was too much and he took his own life.

When it comes to describing the amount of grief and emotional anguish felt by the family, I am truly at a loss for words. The amount of devastation that suicide creates in its path is incalculable. I know this because I am an eyewitness to it. This funeral wasn't just sad or painful, it was tragic. To see a son now fatherless is something that you never forget. As much as his mother, aunts, uncles and grandparents tried to console this boy, they all knew nothing would bring back his father.

This book is about discussing death and dying through the lens of two skateboarders. You knew this when you decided to start reading. We know that suicide is a very difficult topic but feel that it must be discussed. If you or someone you know is having suicidal thoughts, please, stop reading and seek help immediately.

I am not an expert on suicide, but I do know that men, 45 -54 equate to 80% of all suicides in the USA. For those men in this demographic who still skate, I feel it is vital they are aware of this shocking statistic.

From what I have learned, there are 9 key reasons why people take their own life:

Depression
Traumatic stress
Substance abuse
Loss or fear of loss
Hopelessness
Chronic pain and illness
Feeling like a burden to others
Social isolation
Cry for help

I have known four skateboarders who have committed suicide and all but one were in this category. They were all men and I spent quite a bit of time with them. One was Warren Bolster and I've shared with you some of his stories. There was Biker Sherlock — a very famous downhill skater. The third man, unfortunately, is someone I can't write about for reasons of confidentiality.

But the fourth man is someone who I can write about. His name was Martin Streek. Martin was a very well-known Toronto disc jockey and worked for many years at CFNY/The Edge. Our paths crossed because he was into longboarding back in the late 1990's. Martin was a pretty big deal in Toronto and to have him rolling around with my little crew of skaters was quite cool.

After one particularly bad fall, where he shredded his back with road rash, someone managed to take a photo and it appeared in the first edition of *International Longboarder Magazine* (of which I was the founder and co-publisher).

The times that I spent with Martin were pretty wild. He was a pretty intense guy to be with. He had a manic energy that was both amusing and alarming. I think it had something to do with his rock n' roll lifestyle. Oddly enough, we had more than just skateboarding in common.

We were born within 2 months of each other and we both had wide-ranging tastes in music. Although I had at one point in my life spent time working in the music industry, I was nowhere near Martin's level. From here, our similarities started to decrease. When I first met Martin, I was married (for over a decade) and living in suburbia with two kids. Martin, on the other hand, had a bachelor pad downtown. I can't speculate on his relationships, I am quite sure he had several hundred admirers!

In writing this piece, I looked up Martin on the internet. There was of course an immense amount of shock when the news first broke. But tied together with the story was the news that Martin had recently been fired from the radio station where he had dutifully volunteered and worked for 25 years. At the time of his dismissal, CFNY's ratings were suffering. They cleaned house and Martin was the last of the old guard to be sacked.

From the Toronto Star:

Streek's body was found at his apartment on Monday night, two months after he was let go from his 17-year on-air gig at 102.1 The Edge and mere hours after he'd updated his Facebook status with a cryptic and rather foreboding message: "So ... I guess that's it ... thanks everyone ... I'm sorry to those I should be sorry to, I love you to those that I love, and I will see you all again soon (not too soon though) ... Let the stories begin."

"Nobody saw this coming," said Alan Cross, noting that Streek had been pursuing several other projects since parting ways with The Edge.

"I saw him at the Nine Inch Nails/Jane's Addiction show. We sat together. He looked healthy, he looked fine. He looked like I would expect him to look. He was on his way to California to do some white-water rafting with a friend. He said, 'I've got some things planned,' and we just left it at that because he seemed to be okay. And that was the last I saw of him."

Paul Smith, Streek's agent for the past 15 years, was in a similar state of shock.

He spoke with his friend just before he left for California and he was in good spirits. Streek hadn't seemed terribly down about losing his job, either.

"He was so happy and vibrant and comedic and jovial and full of life and laughing and smiling that this is the last thing in the world I would expect Martin Streek to do, to walk off this earth on his own terms," said his friend and fellow Edge announcer Darrin Pfeiffer.

"That's why I'm so shocked. If he got hit by a bus, we'd still be sad, but it'd be like: `Well, that happens. People get hit by buses.' But for him to take his own life, it's now sadness mixed with frustration mixed with a sprinkling of anger … I love him like a brother, but I'm also pissed off at him. I'm pissed off that he would do something like this and leave us all so sad."

An article about Martin by Bert Archer in the Globe and Mail was even more telling. David Marsden, Martin's former boss hinted at one of the possible underlying reasons for his suicide.

This was not unfamiliar territory for Mr. Marsden, who'd been through several firings, a name change, and now works a 10-hours-a-week jockey gig at Oshawa's 94.9 The Rock. "What we are on the radio is what we is," Mr. Marsden says, remembering the last time he saw his old protégé. "When your job disappears, you ask, 'Who am I,' and too often the answer comes back, 'Nobody.'

Men are very much defined by their jobs and careers. When I think about the inner turmoil that Martin was going through as a result of being fired, I am sure it was soul destroying. When we value our job so much that we lose track of relationships, it can be a warning sign.

When it comes to suicide, I think it is the surprise that shocks people the most. They just didn't see it coming. And yet, hindsight can give us some additional clues. Beyond the termination, there was a breakup with a girlfriend that could have added to Martin's anguish (although very little was written about this). Perhaps there were money troubles as projects that Martin thought were coming to fruition, never did. Beyond the 9 reasons, there may have been other factors. All we know is that Martin didn't have an opportunity to deal with his suicidal ideation before it became an actual suicide. That is the tragedy of suicide.

I know that within the next year, I will again be at another funeral that is a result of suicide. I will stand solemnly with the mourners, trying my best to be of support. I will notice their expressions of deep and monumental grief. Like them, I will search in vain for an explanation.

If this article has resonated with you and you know someone who is juggling with one or many of the 9 reasons for suicidal thoughts I urge you to be part of the solution. Take the time to spend time with that person and listen. Just being there for someone can make all the difference between life and death. There are a huge number of resources out there. It is just a question of how to get someone to start the process of seeking help.

Martin Streek was someone who I met through skateboarding and I'll never forget how much I enjoyed just hanging around with him. The truth is that while I only spent a small amount of time with Martin, his death still affects me to this day.

Sudden Death

I'll never forget the first time I met Noel Korman. It was March 11, 2011, and I was at Bustin Boards new longboard shop in New York City. The shop was about to open and it made for the perfect venue to host the world's first longboard expo. We had close to 60 different skate companies show up and it was quite the experience.

It was total pandemonium getting this expo set up. Around 10 o'clock in the morning, in strolled a guy who I'd never seen before. He put out his hand and said in a big, booming voice, "I'm Noel Korman with the Schralper's Union. If you need anything, just let me know." I was floored. Noel had a presence that absolutely lit up the room.

Little did I know what an auspicious moment this would turn out to be. The Schralper's Union was Noel's club for those who did stance sports — skateboarding, snowboarding and surfing. It was all about "spreading high fives and positive vibes." The Union also followed something Noel had developed called "The "Code of the Shralper." It included tenets like, "A Shralper does the right thing because it is the right thing." and "Be prepared to sling stoke in whatever you do, however you do it."

Noel was the kind of person that wouldn't just give you the shirt off his back but a spare bearing, some food and drink and anything you needed. The truth was that Noel didn't have much in this world. Some would say he was generous to a fault. To say he had a larger-than-life personality is a complete understatement.

Noel had spent a number of years selling skateboards and snowboards at one of New York City's best-known sporting goods stores. His goal was to create a fraternity of board sports enthusiasts from locals across the world. In the three years I knew him, we probably only met up half a dozen times. But on every occasion, Noel made such an incredible impression on me and I have such fond memories of the times we spent together.

In the summer of 2012, I found myself at Uncle Funky's skate shop in Greenwich Village. As I walked down the stairs, I could hear Noel's booming voice. He was there with his father, Ray. Curiously enough, I happened to be there with my youngest son, Ethan. For the next two days we spent a huge amount of time hanging out, skating and we even took a road trip to Original Skateboards in New Jersey.

There are so many stories about Noel that they would fill a 500-page book (at least!) I have never met anyone quite like him and I doubt I ever will. Noel was truly one in a million. I could go and on about what a truly remarkable person was, but you get the idea.

In 2014, Noel was trying urgently to make the Schralper's Union successful. He was furiously producing t-shirts, and stickers and spreading the stoke at every event he could attend. As most skaters know, it can be extremely difficult to motivate people into action. But Noel was relentless in trying to establish something of value.

On December 6th of that year, Noel was with his girlfriend, Alice Parks in a New Jersey warehouse. They were working together when the boiler in the building started to malfunction. Tragically, it started to leak carbon monoxide. At the time in the state of New Jersey, carbon monoxide detectors were only mandatory in houses and apartments. The poison leaking from the boiler eventually wound its way to Noel and Alice and they died. What is most horrendous about their deaths is the fact they were entirely preventable.

News of Noel's and Alice's death spread through social media. Ray called me and left one of the most gut-wrenching voicemails I have ever received: "Michael, it's Ray Korman. Noel is dead."

At the funeral, hundreds of Noel's friends turned out. The Shook funeral home normally didn't allow skateboarding in its parking lot, but for that day, they posted a sign that said it was ok. The outpouring of grief on social media was truly breathtaking.

The sudden death of Noel and Alice shocked the East Coast skate community. It was such an unbelievable event and to this day I still find it incomprehensible that Noel and Alice lost their lives this way. Fortunately, as a funeral director's assistant, I have only encountered a handful of deaths that have been sudden. One guy was a lifelong motorcycle enthusiast and he got killed by a car. Another died while canoeing on a lake — he was hit by a jet ski.

In the months following Noel's passing, I became more active in trying to keep his memory alive. I became very close with Ray and tried to support him in any way I could. One of the key things that Ray wanted to see happen was a law that would mandate that all commercial buildings in New Jersey had carbon monoxide detectors. At the time, only houses and apartments needed detectors.

The proposed law was a way to prevent future tragedies. You'd think this law was something of a "no brainer" but somehow, politics got in the way. The Parks/Korman bill was something that Ray was adamant about getting passed in the New Jersey legislature and he worked tirelessly to make it happen. Initially, Ray received a tremendous amount of support and worked with local politicians and the media. But things seemed to get bogged down in the actual passing of the bill.

In the fall of 2015, almost a year after the tragedy, I distinctly recall asking Ray what was happening. I had assumed the bill had passed. It turned out that the New Jersey legislature had indeed signed off on it. But there was one person who was holding things up. The culprit turned out to be Chris Christie — the governor of New Jersey at the time. He was so busy running around trying to get nominated for President that he had yet to sign off on the legislation.

I decided to do something about this situation. I set up an online petition demanding the governor sign off on the bill. I contacted a reporter at a local New Jersey newspaper to drum up some publicity. Almost 1,000 people signed the petition. Chris Christie (or someone in his office) also must have seen what was happening and in November, he eventually signed off on the bill.

The Parks/Korman bill was a key piece of legislation, but it was born from a tragedy. Tragically, adding more grief to this ordeal is the fact that in the months that Chris Christie sat on the bill, an additional 49 people died in New Jersey from carbon monoxide poisoning in buildings that didn't have detectors. These were senseless and completely preventable deaths.

There are no easy answers when it comes to how to deal with sudden death. It's been almost 9 years since Noel died and there is not a week that goes by that I don't think about him. The only thing that comforts me is knowing that the Parks/Korman law will help prevent thousands of more deaths in the decades to come.

Sadly, Ray Korman passed away in 2019. Both are missed.

Life and Rebirth

There's a guy I know named Mike who lives in Texas. We met over 25 years ago when I first started up the SkateGeezer Homepage. He's a very talented artist and he's always struck me as someone who will call BS any time he sees it. I sent him some of the chapters I've written so far. His first take was that he enjoyed some of my anecdotes, but he was still trying to figure out how this book could benefit skaters. He also wondered if I would address what makes skateboarders any different than anyone else facing death or dying. This chapter is my way of addressing these two critical ideas.

Skateboarding has been part of my life for over 45 years. It is something I will always do. In fact, when people ask me if I'll ever stop, I tell them in my deepest Charlton Heston voice "You'll pry this skateboard from my cold dead hands." I am under no delusions, however. I am very aware that I belong to a pretty small constituency — those folks over 50 who still skateboard. I know it's growing, but I get this weird feeling it's a bit like vinyl. Sure, record sales are exploding, but it seems everyone is just streaming music. Plus, pretty much all the record shops have closed where I live.

Nostalgia is something that heavily meshes into skateboarding. But tied into this nostalgia, is a painful boom/bust cycle. When you step back and look at things, both life and rebirth are tied directly into skateboarding.

The '60s were filled with people trying to emulate surfing. Unfortunately, a good many were falling hard on clay wheels. Their injuries became so serious that cities started to ban skateboarding. "The devil's toy" went underground.

The '70s is when I first jumped on a board. Looking back, I'd say my timing was pretty good. The second era of skateboarding was indeed magical. So many critical things were created. The 70's skate boom brought the introduction of the urethane wheel. Things were happening so fast, that every month, dozens of new products were being introduced. Skaters were creating tricks that got more mind-blowing with each edition of SkateBoarder Magazine. It was such an incredible moment in time and then POOF — it was gone. Skate companies folded overnight, skateparks were bulldozed and most people just moved on. I kept at it and wound up being the only skater in my neighborhood.

This boom/bust cycle also resurfaced in the late '80s and mid '90s. A bust hit around in 2018, but the pandemic created a fierce demand for skateboarding. Over three million skaters were added in the USA alone due to COVID. I can't imagine what the Olympics will do for millions of kids worldwide.

I am aware that each generation of skaters has a certain fondness and bias towards their particular time period. It's a heady combination of being young, experiencing freedom and doing something a little dangerous.

But I am also aware that skateboarding has become so incredibly ubiquitous. It's everywhere. Back in the day, if you spotted someone wearing a skate t-shirt or skate shoes, you'd ask if they skated. It was kind of like a secret society. In the time before cell phones, skateboarding wasn't fully underground, but it sure felt like it. Nowadays, if you stop someone who is wearing a Thrasher t-shirt or riding on a longboard or Penny skateboard, they'd think you're very strange. I don't say this to knock these people — but the fact skateboarding has morphed into something very different than when I first started. It's debatable whether the changes within skateboarding have been positive or negative. All I know is that try as you might, you will never stop change and progression from happening within skateboarding — and that's what makes it great.

When I created the SkateGeezer Homepage in 1995, I was thirty-one years old. I am now just a few years away from being almost twice that age. When I go to a skatepark, I know I will be one of two other people over 30 skating — if I am lucky. Most of the time, it's me and a whole bunch of scooter kids. I know they are enjoying themselves and I never want to take anything from their experience, but I know damn well none of them will be riding a scooter at a skatepark at my age.

So, what does this have to do with death and dying and this damn book? First and foremost, I am writing this book for a small audience. I know that some skaters will simply dismiss it. But I also know that it will engage a few of them and get them thinking about death and dying. This is a good thing. Too many people (and especially men) don't want to talk about death and dying. The subject definitely freaks people out. When people avoid talking about death and dying, it can lead to some immense issues. But if this book is able to bring about conversations that lead to concrete action, then it will have all been worthwhile. Consider this book written by skaters, for skaters.

There are now 4 generations of skaters who have experienced the boom/bust cycle of skateboarding. They have seen the "death" of skateboarding and rebirth. Skaters also know that they could die or get seriously injured while they skate. These are all powerful metaphors, seen through the lens of death and dying. Does this mean skateboarders have a unique take on death and dying? I would venture a guess that it really all depends on who the skateboarder is in question.

In truth, I am not qualified to examine why skaters might have a better grip on dealing with death and dying. This is not the reason why I wrote this book and I'll leave it to qualified researchers. I can only go with what I have experienced as a funeral director's assistant and as a skater. So, yes, there is quite a bit of rumination and speculation within the pages of this book. You might not agree with all of it and that's cool.

If you've been rolling around on a board for a few decades and still enjoy it, then kudos to you. If you still get stoked when searching out a new skatepark, then you know the feeling of elation when you take that first ride. I could go on and on about things within skateboarding that bring you joy (the smell of fresh grip tape on a new deck, returning from a heavy session and the look on someone's face as you pump furiously down the sidewalk). The truth is that when you're an older skater, you've made a firm decision to act a little differently. I know that in California there are many skategeezers, so we have to acknowledge that fact. But for most of the other parts of the world, if you're older than 30, you are seen as a bit of an anomaly.

I think the best way to understand what I am trying to say is that you're probably never going to find a book with the title *Badminton, Death, Dying and Spirituality* but I'd be stoked to come across one.

Best Made Plans

Gregg Carroll played a unique role in skateboarding. As part of the first wave, you can catch him in the Academy Award-winning film "Skaterdater." Greg plays the "baddie" in this short (18-minute) film and his skateboarding skills really shine. Shot in 1965, "Skaterdater" is a masterpiece that wonderfully showcases the best aspects of the clay-wheeled era. It's worth viewing on YouTube and chances are you'll wind up repeatedly viewing it — it's that hypnotic!

During my first year as editor of *Concrete Wave*, I was able to contact Gregg and he wrote a lengthy essay detailing his experiences with both the film and life as a pro skater on the Mahaka team. The 60s were indeed a heady time and the surf/skate culture that Gregg was deeply involved with as a pre-teen stayed with him for his entire life.

Like a number of other folks in the skate industry who I have met, I didn't have a great many face to face visits with Gregg. However, the times I spent with him were extremely memorable. He was a very down to earth person along with being very spiritual. I recall one day just hanging out in Dana Point sitting on two chairs discussing life and the afterlife. It was truly an emotional experience that lasted well over 6 hours.

At the time we were sitting in Dana Point, Gregg had been diagnosed with cancer. It was starting to destroy his body, but his mind was still very sharp. Gregg had come to terms with his terminal illness. He had started to reflect on his life and his contributions to skateboarding. It was a privilege to be with him during this time because I knew that time was indeed a very precious commodity for Gregg. Less than a year later, the cancer would take him out.

Tragically, in November of 2013, Gregg Carroll passed away. In May of 2014, he was inducted into the Skateboarding Hall of Fame. The speech that he had written was delivered by his daughter. It was truly amazing to hear his words through her voice. Gregg had prepared every detail with respect to the induction. Eerily, he had a premonition that he was going to be inducted to the Hall of Fame.

For many in the room, there was a sense that Gregg's spirit was there. I'd say he made his presence known by being truly prepared. Although this wasn't a funeral or end of life celebration for Gregg, it sure felt like it. What I took away from it was to write something for my funeral that could be read by family.

This book is meant to spark conversations but I'd also like to give you at least a few ideas that might resonate. Gregg took the time to leave a message to those he left behind. I have attended hundreds of funerals but I have only encountered this idea once. With the right amount of preparation and thought, your voice will reach well beyond the grave. I heard this induction speech over 7 years ago and I can assure you, I will never forget it.

What you decide to put into this farewell address is completely up to you of course. You can add humor, insights or whatever happens to be on your mind at the time you write it. I have my little speech hidden in a container that holds my socks. My brother knows where it is — so if I were to pass unexpectedly, he'll know where to find it.

You also can keep adding to the words or edit out pieces you don't think fit. I suggest revisiting the speech maybe every year or two and keep refining it. Of course, you could write it and be done with it. Just make sure someone other than you knows where to find it.

Gregg's final words to the audience brought everything into focus:
"When those tough days come, when you feel the walls closing in on you a little," he wrote. *"Go jump on your skateboard and feel that special stoke."*

A Wall of Resources

As I mentioned previously, in the final months of publishing *Concrete Wave Magazine*, I got writer's block. Writer's block is no joke. Your creative juices simply stop flowing and you start to panic wondering what on earth you can write about. It was an invisible wall that was truly overwhelming. The problem is you can't seem to get over this wall, no matter what you try. Thankfully, I have conquered this block. But, I have no desire to write a massive book. This is mainly because very few people have the time to read a lot of words. Also, and this is key, I only want to give you the very best of what I have to offer. Filling this book with filler isn't going to help anyone.

I think the idea of a wall provides a perfect metaphor for men and death. While there are some men who have no issues discussing death and dying, for many it is a very difficult subject. They just don't want to consider it or even begin talking about it. It truly remains an invisible wall that seems insurmountable.

You could face this wall alone or with a non-creative approach, but chances are you will never be able to scale it. From what I have experienced, the boost you will need to clear the wall might come from a family member or close friend. Again, if this book provides some positive guidance for a few of my fellow skaters, then that will have been entirely worthwhile.

Thanks to technology, there is a very simple and free way you can start to engage with people about death and dying and start the process of scaling the wall. For example, there are numerous "death cafes" online. This is an informal environment where people can talk about death without any judgment. I have attended a number of these cafes online and I can attest to the power of simply being with others who are sharing their experiences with death and dying. I'd love to see a death cafe which brought together skateboarders.

Rather than looking at a wall as something to be conquered by yourself, recognize that there are many different people who can give you a boost.

From Woo Woo To Wow

My father was raised in quite a religious environment, but towards the end of his life, he moved into the atheist camp. He was a man of medicine and science. While I seem to recall his mother having an inclination towards spirituality, I can affirm that he never showed any remote interest in front of me.

My spiritual journey didn't start until December of 2010. Before that time, I would say I wasn't very spiritual. I enjoyed the social aspect of the religion I was born into, but I was pretty comfortable being very non-observant. Over the past decade or so, there are things that I have experienced that I'd classify as odd or supernatural. So while I am not a big believer in the man or woman upstairs, I am entirely open to the fact that there might be more to this world than what meets the eye. This journey has not been an easy one. When you are hit with a spiritual awakening, it can stress your marriage and your relationships with other family and friends.

I am deeply conflicted when I see stuff online (ie woo woo) that just reeks of being a scam. While prayer can be a huge part of dealing with death and dying, it makes me sick to see people "praying away coronavirus." At the same time, I have personally experienced some excellent meditation sessions via YouTube videos.

So there you have it: I am highly skeptical of what many would call "woo woo," yet I've also personally experienced "wow." Part of my cynicism stems from my father and partially because in the two times I've gone to a psychic, it was total bullshit. I paid my money and just felt they said nothing. I sense this might be several other people's experiences as well. But as I said, in the past ten years, I have also experienced some things that stopped me and made me say, "Wow."

I'll give you an example as to how this conflict between woo-woo and wow runs in my mind. A few weeks before I reached out to Nathan, I had just finished recording a podcast with an interview featuring a sociologist. He had written a book called "Skateboarding and Religion." I started to Google skateboarding and spirituality to find out if there were people I could share this podcast with or if they could be potential interview subjects. This is how I found Nathan.

Turns out that Nathan had posted a comment about this very topic at the website of a skateboarding rabbi. He mentioned he had written a blog post about exactly what I was interested in — skateboarding and spirituality. I clicked and read Nathan's words. They really resonated. Ironically the date of the post was 11/08/2013. I was born on August 11 (08/11). When I mentioned this to Nathan, I was told that he'd actually written the post on November 8! As you can see, it's pretty easy to go from Wow to woo woo, too.

For right now, I am trusting in the process. So far, it hasn't let me down. I am very glad that I got in contact with Nathan. I sense I have much to learn from him.

The question then is how does one move from woo-woo to wow? If you're reading all parts of this book, then you're also experiencing what Nathan has written. If you're a bit skeptical, you might find yourself questioning what he's written. At the same time, I think there is a part of us that wants to explore the areas of spirituality, free of judgment or prejudice. The question is can we allow ourselves to do this? I am hoping this book provides an opportunity.

One of the best things about skateboarding at my age is that most young people don't perceive me as a skater. Like pretty much everyone, they judge a book by its cover. I am proud of the fact that I don't look like a skater but still have the mentality of a skater. Sure, I don't have the same abilities as I once had, but I am still down to skate and do it at every opportunity I can find.

The same thing happens when I discuss spirituality. I have spent a lot of time researching things like chakras, but I don't look like the type of person who would do this. I know that sounds pretty prejudicial, but prior to December of 2010, I was very judgmental of people who mentioned the word chakras. I thought it was woo-woo.

It is this feeling of non-judgment that is the best approach when it comes to spiritual matters. There are dozens of modalities or paths within spiritual experiences. It all comes down to what really resonates with you personally. You have to be honest with yourself, and this can be difficult. I sincerely hope that as Nathan and I journey together in a voyage of discovery we will be able to accomplish more than if we'd done it alone. I feel comfortable questioning everything but will also acknowledge when something has moved me to say, "Wow!"

A few people ask if I've seen ghosts or spirits either at the funeral home or in the back of the coach. The short answer is no. The longer answer is still no.

Things Said And Not Said

Perhaps one of the more challenging parts of my job is to be present at an ID. An ID is when the deceased is lying in the casket in the back of the coach and the family requests to view the body. This takes place during the start of a funeral. Holding up an umbrella for privacy, we carefully lift open the casket, and the family is free to share any last words or to simply gaze at the face of their loved one.

To see grief this close and personal every week requires a certain mindset. While I have no connection to the people who are in mourning, I can empathize with them. Although I have done this many times, you never know what to prepare for. I'd like to share with you one experience that took place over two years ago but will forever be seared into my memory.

The parents had divorced, and the children were in their early to mid-teens. Tragically, the ex-husband had overdosed on drugs. I seem to recall he was in his mid 40's. From what I could understand, drugs had shattered the marriage and most of the relationships with the children. At the casket, there was truly a feeling of dread and regret. Dread, because I sense that both family and friends had a gut feeling this day was coming and regret because they all felt powerless to stop it from happening.

As the tears flowed, the family tried to support each other through this remarkably difficult time. The children dropped letters into the casket and spoke to the father about how they felt about his death. It was truly a raw and visceral experience that I will never forget.

I started to think about what the children said and wrote to their late father while at the casket. While I truly wished that somehow he could hear and read these heartfelt sentiments, I knew that was just wishful thinking. The man was dead, and whatever had been said while he was alive seemed to have very little bearing on the outcome. I will never know what the family said or wrote to this man while he was alive. All I experienced was the grief and anger that they displayed now that he was no longer there. Fortunately, I don't see many IDs like the one I've just described.

The time for real talk is not when someone is dead. That is merely a one-way conversation.

The Real Bucket List

Most likely, you've heard about the bucket list — the list of things that people wish to accomplish before they die. Many of these lists consist of visiting specific places and doing special things. They can range from the pretty cool (hold a shark in Hawaii) to the completely ridiculous (hold a dangerous snake around your neck...I assuming in Hawaii)

I encourage everyone I know to make a bucket list. Skaters worldwide have numerous places and experiences that they could add to such a list. Just as a start, consider the following: hit the ditches of New Mexico, visit the skateparks of Colorado, and take part in New York's Broadway Bomb.

I think a bucket list is something that, for most people, is aspirational and exciting but can also be financially challenging. I am here not to burst your bubble. I merely want to point out that sometimes life gets in the way of your plans.

As I write these words, I hope I've got just under four more years of full-time work. I say hope because you never know what could happen. I have my health, but I don't have the finances to fully retire. I know I'll get there soon because I realize it's a marathon, not a sprint. I have some key places I'd like to visit with my wife, but I am well aware of the fact that we BOTH have to be in good shape to accomplish them. So while I've been working, I've been focusing my attention on the real bucket list.

What is the real bucket list? The REAL bucket list consists of just ONE item. But this item is so critical that it supersedes all the other items and lists. Oftentimes when I am at a funeral, I will learn about the many trips that the deceased went on with their spouse. Or I'll learn about the volunteer work that the person did. The most popular thing I hear from grandchildren concerns the amount of time they spend with their grandparents. These stories are always touching when you hear them because you know that the time put into building and strengthening these relationships transcends time. The memories are all you have left when a person passes.

The real bucket list is about spending time with the people you love and care deeply about. Creating memories in some far-off place you've wanted to visit is an admirable goal. You start to see patterns when you hear as many eulogies as I do. I can almost instantly tell by how a family grieves what kind of parents or grandparents the deceased were. If the time was put into generating thousands of memories, you can just feel it.

Please understand that I don't want to take anything from bucket lists. It's important to have goals and dreams. But while you are waiting for the clock to run down on your life as an employee and begin retirement, many things can happen.

As you get older, there are moments when you reflect on decisions you've made. These are things that you've done or in some cases, not done. I think you can gain quite a bit of insight from these reflections, but I believe it is important to frame them correctly and limit the number of times you do this. Castigating yourself for a poor decision can lead to bitterness and depression.

Often, people will blame themselves for a job offer not taken or a financial decision that didn't quite pan out. One of my co-workers could have bought an apartment complex in Toronto in the late 1970's for under $50,000. It's probably worth over $3,000,000 today. He constantly reminds me of this painful mistake.

He has a bucket list of places he wants to visit. He's got the money, and if he wants, he could retire tomorrow, but his wife doesn't want to travel. They've been married for decades, but I suspect they haven't really been on the same page for a long time.

I knew a man who spent over 35 working hard building a business. After decades of struggle, he finally became financially successful, and in his mid-50's he decided to retire. He and his wife bought a beautiful new house. They started to travel, and life was going exceptionally well. Unfortunately, less than two years after his decision to retire, he had liver cancer and passed at the age of 57.

But this is not the entire story. The sad truth is that in the decades he'd worked, he sacrificed much time with his family. The relationship with his son and daughter was not very healthy. I look at the real bucket list as an insurance policy. No matter what life throws at you, if you've invested the time with family and friends, you will never have any regrets.

Don't take my word for it; look at the top bucket list items from USA Today.

Look what is in the number one position. That's what happens when you invest time in family and friends.

Change someone's life for the better — 52%
Get to my ideal weight — 47%
Go on a safari — 45%
Ride a hot air balloon — 45%
See the Northern Lights — 45%
Go to the Super Bowl — 43%
Swim with dolphins — 39%
Travel through Europe — 38%

THE ENDLESS WAVE | PART ONE

While You Can Still Push

Today we buried a 99-year-old woman. This is not a common occurrence. Most people don't live this long, and oftentimes, people who live to almost 100 have outlived most of their friends and immediate family. But what made this burial even more of a unique experience was that the woman lost her husband in 1976. This means she was in her mid-50s when she experienced this tragedy.

When I was first at the grave taking a GPS (so that future visitors could locate it), I met up with the daughter. She first said to me that her mother had wanted to die. The daughter was absolutely adamant that her mother wanted to depart this world. I knew that was a bittersweet admission, which is not uncommon for me to hear. "My mother was the most intelligent person I've met," she remarked. "She knew that her time had come, and I am glad she's on her way to see my dad."

As I stared at the husband's gravestone, I started to think. This woman went more than half her life without her spouse. My first thoughts were, "Wow, what a huge loss, How on earth did her family cope? It must have been so terribly awful for her." I thought about how lonely she might have been. I wondered about finances. I am pretty sure you thought the same thing. But the reality of her life, thanks to some very illuminating eulogies from her son and grandchildren, was completely different from what I expected.

The son started out by saying that her mother had many male companions. Not one or two, but many. He made a point of saying that his mother had lots of relationships after her husband had died. Some in the crowd laughed at this remark and could see smiles. Obviously, the death of her husband didn't stop her from loving other men. I think that speaks volumes. On top of this, it turned out that her husband actually ran his own business. As soon as he passed away, she was now thrust into the role of owner. From what I understand, she took over the reins with great success. She ran the company for seven years, and eventually, it was sold.

I started to think how old the children were when their father died. Probably in their mid-twenties. How devastating that must have been. And yet, at the funeral, I witnessed many loving tributes from grandchildren and great-grandchildren.

A life that is cut short at a pretty young age can have a horrendous impact on a family. I was 54 in 2018. So much has happened in these past three years. I know that sounds rather odd, but is true. There's something about being a man over the age of 50. Health issues seem to crop up, and as I wrote in a previous chapter, stuff that you haven't handled will creep up on you mightily.

Death has a way of completely changing people. Some become more religious, others start a whole new career path, and others focus more on what really counts.

I can't say for certain that there isn't intergenerational trauma in this family. I am not sure what ghosts lurk in the closets. But I can say that this woman is a pretty amazing example of getting on with the business of living.

Throughout this book, we hope to give you a perspective of death and dying through the lens of skateboarding. Much has been written about "seizing the day." The old chestnut of "not counting every day but making every day count" seems to buzz through my brain weekly.

As skaters, we have to make every day count. Especially in the icy cold winter when we can't get out there and ride. The winter might stop you from skateboarding, but it won't be permanent while you can still push.

THE ENDLESS WAVE | PART ONE

The Magic Of Balance

It was a Saturday evening, and it was my team's turn to come in and do our shift here at the funeral home. Our Saturday night shift starts pretty late in the summer months, and this one was no exception. As I peered into the main office at 9:40 p.m.. I looked at the possible incoming transfers that we would need to handle. A transfer is usually from someone's residence, hospital bed or morgue. Sometimes, we have to pick up bodies from the coroner. This means the death is suspicious. Usually, it's an accidental death or a suicide.

As I glanced at the paperwork, I was astonished to see someone I knew had passed away, and his body was at the coroner. Immediately, I feared the worst. I sensed it was a suicide. Not only was this person someone I knew, I had written a story about him and printed it in a magazine I published back in 2015. For confidential reasons, I will just call him "Bill"

Bill was a professional magician, and I met him back in 2015 as he was performing his tricks at a friend's 50th birthday party. When you see a roaming magician at a party, you enjoy the momentary show and get back to conversing with your friends. But something magical happened when I met Bill. It turned out we were a year apart in age, and oddly enough, he was as intrigued by skateboarding as much as I love magic. Over the course of the evening, we spent some additional time chatting. I think I enjoyed watching people's reactions to his presentation more than he did.

At the time of our meeting, I was publishing a magazine called *Untapped*. It was about finding your flow and the concept of serendipity. Let's just say it was a bit out there and probably way ahead of its time. But Bill was a perfect fit for the magazine. I knew instinctively that I wanted to do a profile on him. So, we exchanged emails and arranged for a time to meet up. His apartment was bursting with boxes of magic tricks, and we spent a great deal of time talking about the power of magic.

Bill offered me a glimpse into his life as a professional magician, and I shared with him what it was like being a skateboard magazine publisher. Initially, I would have given anything to trade places with him, but as I got to know him, I sensed some struggles were bubbling under the surface. My wife always says I am a pretty bad judge of character, but in this particular case, I had a feeling that when Bill quit the corporate world to do magic, it hadn't been an easy ride. I could sense some demons were brewing under the surface.

When Bill expressed a desire for a skateboard, I procured one for him. I vividly recall teaching him how to ride it. He was a little nervous and was worried about falling on his hands. But Bill tried his best, and I know that he was stoked with the skateboard I gave him. Sadly, my goal of learning a card trick that I purchased was not as successful. Despite having the instructions, it seemed that only a practiced magician like Bill could make the trick work. The preparation and presentation were way above my level.

Although ours was a brief friendship, it was one of the most unique experiences I have encountered. Magicians like Bill are literally in a world of their own making, and we are, for the most part, spectators watching their show.

Bill spent countless hours perfecting his magic routine, and he had quite an intense demeanour. But he also had a big heart and loved to share the joy of magic with anyone he met. Bill also spent a lot of time working with schools teaching magic to kids. He used magic to explain science and math, which blew their minds. In fact, some of his tricks were so good that I borrowed them and integrated them into a programme that I created called "The Magic of

Balance." For a few years, I taught students balancing skills through skateboarding (and stilts!) along with magic tricks.

When I saw Bill's name on the transfer board, I was shocked and deeply saddened. I am not sure exactly how he died, but I sense that behind Bill's gregarious personality, some deeper issues finally caught up with him. Entertainers give so much of themselves that sometimes they get lost in the mix. What pains me the most is that Bill sacrificed so much to become a magician. Here's what I wrote in the article, *"I've sacrificed a lot to be a magician. I don't eat in fancy restaurants, and I traded in my car. The biggest payoff is not financial, it is what I do for people."*

Further on in the piece, Bill says, *"I am truly honoured and grateful to have this ability to make someone smile or forget their problems for just a brief moment."* Reading the feature six years later fostered so many different memories and emotions. Ironically enough, there's a guy I work with who actually went to high school with Bill. They played on the same sports teams together. Like me, he is deeply saddened by Bill's passing.

The outpouring of grief and sadness expressed on the virtual guestbook on our website is immense. There are literally dozens of people writing their condolences. Here are a few that are of particular note:

Bill taught me never to accept the ordinary. Never stop taking risks in the pursuit of what you love. I will forever be grateful to him.

What a huge personality and that smile...it could melt ice. You couldn't help but be inspired by Bill's personality and gift of magic. The world has lost a genuinely kind soul.

He brought so much happiness to so many people with his magic, including our children. His passion for the arts, whether it was his magic, photography or playing the guitar, was both inspirational & admirable. There were no half-measures with Bill, he was all in. His presence and smile lit up every room he entered, leaving us all feeling loved and cared for.

There is a great deal of talk these days about mental health issues. Back in 1975, when I started skateboarding, topics like depression and anxiety were not discussed publicly. Over the past 45 years or so, there has been a change. But there is still much work to do. His devotion to magic kept the demons and issues that plagued Bill at bay. But sadly, these problems will not magically disappear on their own by sheer force or evasion. I've often said that skateboarding provided me (and still provides me) with both a creative and emotional outlet. But when I really think about things, skateboarding has really provided me with the magic of balance

The List

Thus far, I've probably attended well over 500 funerals in my three years working at the funeral home. The truth is, it's all become a bit of a blur. There are days when I work at three funerals. I don't want to sound callous or indifferent, but I must acknowledge my feelings. The fact is that working in the deathcare field is unlike anywhere else I've ever worked. Yes, I know it's a business, but an emotional component far exceeds anything you read about or see in films. Sometimes I can become emotional at a funeral, but it is quite rare. The fact is I am there to support family and friends in a very painful experience. This is where I find my humanity — in the service of others.

I decided to compile a list of people I have met through skateboarding who have passed away. Most of these people I either worked with professionally (as a publisher or writer) or spent some time with. All were skateboarders and left a huge mark on the sport. Some were friends, some could be challenging to hang with, and all were unforgettable.

Gregg Carroll — Co-star of SkaterDater film (60)
Fausto Vitello — founder of Thrasher (age 59)
Warren Bolster -editor of SkateBoarder Magazine (age 59)
Ty Page — skate legend (age 59)
Wee Willi Winkels — skate inventor (age 56)
Don "Waldo" Autry — skate legend (age 55)

Shogo Kubo — skate legend (age 54)
Jay Adams — skate legend (age 53)
Brad Edwards — longboard pioneer (age 49)
Biker Sherlock — downhill champion/owner Dregs Skateboards (age 47)
Martin Streek — radio disk jockey at CFNY (age 45)
Noel Korman — founder of The Shralpers Union (39)

As I add up the total number of names, I find myself stunned into silence. Even typing these words feels a little surreal. Truly, this is not an exercise for the faint of heart. I seriously cannot believe how many people I've known who have died at such an early age.

Do I recommend you compile a list? This is entirely up to you. If you do decide to compile a list of people who you met through skateboarding who are no longer around, be prepared to be shocked.

If there is a silver lining to this exercise, it rests with the fact that despite their fairly young age, these individuals made a huge difference in the world. For this, we can all be grateful.

Difficult People & Death

In the summer of 2021, I arrived along with my two other teammates at a stunning house on an extremely fancy street. I'd say the house was probably worth well north of 7 million dollars — and that's not including all the art inside. It was a planned death or what we would also call a medically assisted death. These calls are generally peaceful. While there is sadness in the air, there is also relief.

We carefully maneuvered around the sculptures and transferred the woman out of the house. We spoke very little and had just a brief interaction with the family. Within 10 minutes, we were on our way back to the funeral home.

The next day, about 25 people showed up for the funeral. There was only one speaker, and he was not part of the family. His eulogy went on for almost thirty minutes. If I could pick two words to describe it, I'd choose "brutally authentic." While I had never had the chance/misfortune to meet this woman, she seemed like a real piece of work.

We have all encountered "difficult" or "challenging" people. These descriptions are just euphemisms. More often than not, we simply call these people bitches, bastards or assholes. Some seem to take great pleasure in other's pain. We all have bad days, but these people have perpetual bad months, years, decades and lifetimes.

I'd venture a guess that, sadly, many suffer from depression and mental illness, all stemming from trauma. Unfortunately, they have never received appropriate treatment. Perhaps the therapy they did receive didn't work. This is highly problematic because they make everyone else's life a living hell.

How much of a pain in the ass was this deceased woman? During the eulogy, the clergyperson called her a complainer and difficult along with being extremely challenging. He implored people to remember the positive aspects of her, even if there was only one. Repeatedly he asked people to not dwell on the past and move forward. He also thanked people for coming, adding that he knew it might be difficult for some to attend the funeral. I'd say this guy earned his paycheck that day!

Imagine what kind of legacy you've left that no family member is prepared to talk about you at your funeral, and you have to be thanked for just showing up.

I am quite sure psychiatrists could spend hours dissecting this insane eulogy. It completely blew my mind. But then again, this is the legacy of difficult people. The old saying goes, "People don't remember what you say or do, they remember how you made them feel." Judging by this woman's eulogy, I'd say she made people feel like crap most of the time.

Sadly, making people feel like crap can be quite easy if you're not careful. I'd be lying if I hadn't done it myself. So, I will not sit here in a glass house and throw stones. For the most part, though, I've tried not to be an asshole. I'll admit I am still a work in progress.

But this woman seemed to have taken things to a whole new level. Her legacy was probably set in motion decades ago and sadly, she never felt the need to change. That's the most frustrating thing about difficult people — they are either lost in a fog of their own rage/frustration/emotional baggage, or they are completely aware they are jerks and don't wish to change.

As publisher and editor of *Concrete Wave*, I had the chance to meet with many people in skateboarding. I met people at the beginning of their careers in the industry, along with the biggest stars. There were all types of personality types, from the kind and generous to the narcissistic dick. But this book is not a tell-all about who's a nice guy and who's an asshole. I'll let someone else write about that. It is, however, a book about death and dying. So, I will mention two particular people who were difficult, heavily involved in skateboarding and are both dead. Both people were difficult and ventured into asshole territory many times. Since neither of these people can defend themselves, I will keep their names private and the descriptions mercifully short.

The first person seemed to relish berating people and was constantly in a state of agitation. For some reason, he took great pleasure in making my life difficult — and he loved trying to embarrass me in front of my peers. His ego was enormous, and he was literally a living troll. Eventually, things caught up with him and his business collapsed.

I got to meet up with him when he lost his business. He was trying to make a comeback. We went for a sushi lunch, and he was much more subdued — dare I say humbled? He seemed more at peace, and we had a rather enjoyable lunch. But in the back of my mind, I couldn't help but think that if he hadn't lost his business, would he be acting like this? I know the answer, but I keep that luncheon as my primary memory of him because less than 12 months later, he was dead.

The second person was someone whom I had known for over 25 years. I had met him in the mid-80s skateboarding outside a music club. I watched as he grew his business from literally a table in the back of a bike shop to a huge retail colossus. He had a reputation for being fairly nasty to customers. What made him behave in such a way? I am pretty sure he was bipolar. The stigma of mental illness is still an issue, but twenty or thirty years ago, it was huge, and it was most certainly the elephant in the room.

While I have mostly positive memories of this person, he could be very prickly. At one point, he told me to shove my magazine up my ass. A few years later, he phoned me to apologize. The apology seemed genuine, but I was still extremely puzzled about why he would call. Within a few years of this call, he would wind up like person number one — dead. I have decided to keep that phone call as my primary memory of him.

Thankfully, I've heard only a few eulogies that are brutally authentic. They are similar to driving past a car crash. You tell yourself you don't want to look, but you seem oddly compelled. I know that many people can understand the need to air dirty laundry in public. If there is someone in your life who was difficult, and you now have to say something at the funeral (and gathering), you are faced with quite a challenge.

It can feel cathartic to really let things go, and airing dirty laundry means that your exact feelings are well known. Perhaps too well-known! Conversely, you could keep things on a positive note but this might diminish your true feelings. Keeping skeletons in closets has its advantages, but sometimes they need to be evicted.

I suggest there are a few other choices you could make. For example, you could say nothing and politely decline any offer to speak. Your silence can speak volumes. You can get extremely creative and speak in metaphors and hints. This turns the eulogy into more of a mystery, and it runs the risk of confusing people. But then again, those in the know will know, and everyone else will just think you were being creative.

In the final analysis, the person is dead, and you are not. Beyond the funeral and the eulogy, I'd say when it comes to difficult people who have made your life hell, living well is the best revenge.

Regret

Two things happened to me during the time I was writing this book and I felt the urgency to add them. One event left me with what you could call a sting of regret, while the other made me realize just how difficult regret can be to manage.

The first one probably happened to you somehow — I got ripped off, but it was for a small amount. It was time for lunch, and I eagerly entered a local pizza joint. I carefully gazed up at the menu, trying to figure out the best value for my dollar. You've probably experienced this. You are trying to determine the ratio of how much pizza could three people eat vs. how much you want to pay.

Taking a moment, I determined that an extra large with three toppings was going to do the job and dutifully paid my $33 bill. It seemed a little excessive, but I pulled out my credit card nonetheless. "Come back in 15 minutes," the pizza maker said. I then went outside to buy some orange juice at the variety store just around the corner. When I returned to the pizza place, I happened to notice a large sign on the other part of the entrance that said 1 medium 1 topping pizza — $8.99. It turned out that my non-diligence had cost me at least $10 extra dollars.

As I picked up the pizza, I told the guy, "I guess two mediums would have sufficed — maybe next time." I felt ripped off. Instead of providing me with some guidance, he was content to take the money and bake. I know it was a small thing, but damn, I was filled with regret. I should have been more careful!

I know that this feeling will eventually dissipate, and I'll eventually encounter another egregious display of greed. That's just the way things work. While I am filled with regret at this pizza purchase, and I blame myself for not being more vigilant, I recognize that in the grand scheme of things, it won't make or break me.

But there are regrets that we sometimes carry throughout our lives and all the way to our deathbeds. These are not just regrets that sting but leave a deep hole.

I encountered a conversation yesterday with a friend that featured a number of deep regrets. While this person is nowhere near his deathbed, he has carried these regrets for decades. I sense they are for him very much like luggage on a carousel that you find at the airport. The baggage continuously revolves in his mind. A number of his regrets involve decisions not taken — especially when it came to business opportunities. "I could have bought some real estate in the mid-70s in Toronto, but I was advised not to. That place would have brought in millions in revenue, and it would be worth a fortune now."

Here's another one: "I should have quit the job when they started to treat me like crap, but I never did." Once his carousel started spinning, it never seemed to stop. There was a flood of regret and sorrow for decisions not taken. I tried to comfort my friend. I listened, but in the back of my mind, I was thinking, "Holy crap, I am glad I have the ability to let go." Eventually, I had to get back home. But the depth of this man's regret weighed heavily on me. It still does.

Bonnie Ware is an Australian nurse caring for numerous people on their deathbeds. She came up with a list of five of the biggest regrets of the dying, and it became a wildly popular blog post and eventually a book. I share them with you now, hoping you get a chance to reflect on what's important.

1. I wish I'd had the courage to live a life true to myself, not the life others expected of me.
"This was the most common regret of all. When people realize that their life is

almost over and look back clearly on it, it is easy to see how many dreams have gone unfulfilled. Most people had not honoured even a half of their dreams and had to die knowing that it was due to choices they had made or not made. Health brings a freedom very few realize until they no longer have it."

2. I wish I hadn't worked so hard.
"This came from every male patient that I nursed. They missed their children's youth and their partner's companionship. Women also spoke of this regret, but as most were from an older generation, many of the female patients had not been breadwinners. All of the men I nursed deeply regretted spending so much of their lives on the treadmill of a work existence."

3. I wish I'd had the courage to express my feelings.
"Many people suppressed their feelings in order to keep peace with others. As a result, they settled for a mediocre existence and never became who they were truly capable of becoming. Many developed illnesses relating to the bitterness and resentment they carried as a result."

4. I wish I had stayed in touch with my friends.
"Often, they would not truly realize the full benefits of old friends until their dying weeks, and it was not always possible to track them down. Many had become so caught up in their own lives that they had let golden friendships slip by over the years. There were many deep regrets about not giving friendships the time and effort that they deserved. Everyone misses their friends when they are dying."

5. I wish that I had let myself be happier.
"This is a surprisingly common one. Many did not realize until the end that happiness is a choice. They had stayed stuck in old patterns and habits. The so-called 'comfort' of familiarity overflowed into their emotions, as well as their physical lives. Fear of change had them pretending to others, and to themselves, that they were content, when deep within, they longed to laugh properly and have silliness in their life again."

This book is not here to counsel you through regret. For that, you're going to need a therapist or at least a few hours reading about how to deal with it. But like I've said, this book is meant to be a catalyst. If this book has exposed you to these 5 critical ideas, and you decide to make a course correction in your life, that's great.

When I think about my time in the skate industry, I have to be honest when it comes to assessing how things went. I made thousands of decisions in almost 25 years. From the decision to write a piece on my skateboarding experiences for the Dansworld website to eventually letting go of the magazine, I can say there were only a few things I regret doing or not doing. Thankfully, with the passage of time, the sting of these regrets has either faded out or disappeared entirely.

When I look at the decisions I've made throughout my 50-plus years, I am proud to say that I rarely stand near the baggage carousel.

As you wander into the worlds of death and dying, you may very well encounter the "R" word. Regret is a double-edged sword. Sometimes, it is the path NOT taken that makes all the difference in the world.

I think this quote from William Shatner is probably the best way to look at regret. *"Regret is the worst human emotion. If you took another road, you might have fallen off a cliff. I'm content."*

The Who What, Where, When, Why and How of Death

During the writing of this book, I have strived to weave my life as a skater with a glimpse of what the world of death is like. I know that some will find this an extremely difficult juxtaposition to deal with. I admit it, it is jarring. But I also have to say that knowledge is power and hopefully, this book has given you a little bit more power.

I feel quite confident this power will be very useful in navigating the waters of death and dying. My sense is that you will be able to use the health/deathcare system to help and support you, rather than scrambling and trying to figure out what exactly is happening. Make no mistake, the health/death care industry is complex and formidable. A misstep can lead to a great deal of unnecessary problems.

When you are thrust into a situation that you are unfamiliar with, it can cause panic and irrational decision making. If this book does anything, I really hope that it has acted as a catalyst for you to get prepared.

Please note that the statistics quoted in this piece are geared to North America, Europe and Australia. They are approximations and averages. As they say, your mileage may vary.

WHO IS GOING TO DIE?
You. You are going to die.

WHAT WILL KILL ME?
A number of things. But the number one thing that will kill you is your heart. Heart disease is a huge killer — everywhere. The technical term is ischaemic heart disease. Here's how you can avoid it:

1. Be physically active — get out there and skate!
2. Manage your diabetes (if you have it)
3. Maintain a healthy cholesterol level — reduce fats in your diet
4. Keep a normal blood pressure
5. Don't smoke

WHAT ABOUT CANCER?
It's number 2 with a bullet.

WHAT ELSE WILL KILL ME?
Dementia and Alzheimer's are at number 3. If you don't want to die from these two, do the following:

- Be physically active.
- Eat healthily.
- Don't smoke.
- Drink less alcohol.
- Exercise your mind.
- Take control of your health.

It's pretty interesting that the same things that will prevent heart disease also prevent dementia. If you're beginning to see a pattern here, you can carry it on through the rest of this article. The more you follow these 6 guidelines, the better chances your body will be healthy and the longer you will live.

ANYTHING ELSE GONNA KILL ME?
Having a stroke along with lung disease. Lung disease falls into the category of chronic obstructive pulmonary disease. These are things like emphysema and bronchitis. If you don't want to die from this, don't smoke.

IS THAT ALL?
No. Lower respiratory infections, colon and rectum cancers, kidney disease, hypertensive heart disease and diabetes.

As someone who reads a great many death certificates (this note explains the cause of death), I can definitely attest that this list is accurate. You will die eventually, but you can help prolong your life by following the steps outlined in this piece. There, I've said it twice.

WHERE AM I GOING TO DIE?
Believe it or not, this is a rather difficult question to answer. When I started researching this question it became apparent that answering it depends on which country you live in and what kind of health issues you are facing. In Canada, almost 60% of deaths occur in hospitals and 40% are in people's homes. In the USA, there is a growing trend of people dying at home.

In many polls, respondents have overwhelmingly said they wanted to die at home. The reasons for this are many, but I think it boils down to familiarity and being with loved ones. Unfortunately, the reality of caring for a dying person in a home can be very complex and incredibly stressful. Your family becomes your caregivers full time. This doesn't allow for any other type of relationship and this can be extremely hard.

If you or a loved one have a terminal illness, I highly recommend looking into hospice. Before he passed, my father was in a hospital for a month. He received great treatment but it was loud and sterile. He was uncomfortable. The hospice was peaceful and tranquil. If I had to choose between dying in a hospice or a home, I'd choose a hospice every time.

WHEN AM I GOING TO DIE?
Like the previous question, this is a matter of geography. About 300,000 people die each year in Canada. The average life expectancy for men in Canada is 80. For women, it is 84. But if you go south, to the USA, men's life expectancy drops to 75 and 80 to women.

Here are some more numbers to gaze upon:
Ages 60 — 64 = 7% of all deaths
Ages 65 — 69 = 11% of all deaths
Ages 70 — 74 = 17% of all deaths
Ages 75- 79 = 28% of all deaths
Ages 80 — 84 = 50% of all deaths
Ages 85 — 89 = 88% of all deaths

You have less than a 2% chance of living to 100. I have been at several funerals of people who reach this age (and over it — one lady was 104!).

WHY AM I GOING TO DIE?
Well, you're human. Shit happens and we eventually die. Fate. Karma. Health issues. Family genes. Stress. Smoking. Alcohol. Lack of exercise. I could go on and on, but you get the idea.

HOW AM I GOING TO DIE?
Hopefully, you will heed my advice and start to really think about what you want. There are numerous websites that offer ideas and plans on death and dying. Here are just a few:

https://www.dyingmatters.org/
http://www.orderofthegooddeath.com/
https://www.artofdyingwell.org/
https://www.dyingwithdignity.ca/

A Celebration of Life

Willi Winkels was truly both a skate pioneer and a legend. You might not know his name, but if you ride a laminated skateboard, you have him to thank. Willi Winkels did a huge amount for action sports and most sadly, riders are blissfully unaware. I wrote four pages about him in my book *The Concrete Wave*. While he is famous for creating the first laminated skateboard decks, he also ventured off into lots of other areas too. Willi was a pioneer in the world of snowboarding and actually invented the word "snowboard."

My earliest memory of Willi was his skate team coming to my hometown of London, Ontario back in 1977. This was a major contest, and Willi had his amazing demo team out in full force. To my impressionable mind, watching Willi was an absolutely life-changing event. He rode all kinds of boards, including a gas-powered longboard and an eight-wheeler. The team was made up of skaters a little older than me and I was seriously jealous of them.

Willi promoted skateboarding and snowboarding for many decades. He was also a pioneer in wakeboarding. He also invented mobile half pipes and a portable cassette player well before Sony came out with the Walkman. The cigarette lighter powered by the sun was pure genius too!

When it came time to interview him for *The Concrete Wave* book, he was very gracious with his time. It was 1997 and 20 years had passed since I had seen him in London. He greeted me with a big smile, a beverage in hand while wearing a bathrobe. My first thought was that he was definitely channeling his inner Lebowski.

Willi had some amazing stories about his time working in the skate industry and it was especially fascinating to hear about his business relationship with Tom Sims. I invited Willi to my book launch back in 1999 and it felt like I was back in London all those years ago. We held the launch at a skatepark and I think Willi enjoyed doing the skate demo as much as I loved being a first-time author.

Over the next two decades or so, Willi and I remained in contact. A few times a year he'd call me with an idea he had for skateboarding or he'd ask a question about the industry. I tried my best to help out. I got the sense he was THIS close to launching something truly wonderful, but nothing seemed to really gel.

At the beginning of 2014, I received a call from Willi. His voice wasn't the same and I had a feeling something was up. It turned out he had cancer. He was anxious to get some of his stories recorded and he wondered if I would come up to Collingwood and interview him. I quickly arranged for a team to join me. We met Willi in a retirement home where he was trying to recover from the treatment. It was here that I got to know Willi's wife, Judy. She was devastated by what Willi was experiencing. They had been together since they were in their teens and Judy knew that losing Willi was going to be extremely painful.

I spent a few hours interviewing Willi and hoped that he would recover. But he looked very frail and I sensed that he didn't have much time. By the time March rolled around, Willi had died at the age of 58.

My attention turned to Judy and I tried to support her as best as I could. She was overwhelmed by grief. She hadn't only lost her husband, she had lost her best friend. Over the next few months, we started to think about a tribute party for Willi. As we began planning the event, I could tell that it was a therapeutic experience for Judy. I was also grateful that I was able to celebrate the life of someone who had contributed to the sport I love so much.

In September of 2014,, we hosted a huge party in honor of Willi at Blue Mountain Ski Resort. Besides snowboarding, Willi was an avid skier and he actually has a run named for him at the resort. Hundreds of friends and family paid heartfelt tributes to Willi. The stories that were shared were truly special. We hired a Beatles cover band that brought down the house. It was truly an epic event. I can honestly say that it was a privilege just to be there and help plan it.

If you ever find yourself in the position of creating a tribute to someone who has died or you can assist with a celebration of life ceremony, I strongly encourage you to take part. It's been almost seven years since this event. While it was indeed bittersweet, I am so glad I was a part of it.

Fast forward to 2023. I am now older than the age that Willi passed. It is staggering to think how much he accomplished in his brief time on this planet. He definitely needs to be part of the Skateboarding Hall of Fame.

A Planned Death

Here in Canada, medical assistance in death (MAID) is legal. At this point, it only accounts for less than 2% of all deaths. But, the numbers are growing. There is a huge amount of information available on the web about this subject. Depending on where you live, it could be either completely outlawed or 100% legal.

From what I have seen in my role as a funeral director's assistant, people who decide they do not wish to continue living are grateful for the opportunity to make such a decision. The places where I have picked up the deceased are tranquil and peaceful. Family members are both upset and relieved. Overall the feeling that I get is one of peace.

This might strike some readers as odd. How can there be peace if the person has given up at least trying to fight for his or her life? I think that many baby boomers are putting quality of life above quantity of life. They have seen what happened with their parents and many are not prepared to go through the same experiences.

The reality is that baby boomers changed child rearing, education, music, film and politics (to name just a few things). I sense that death will be no exception. The oldest baby boomer turned 75 in 2021. The vast majority are entering their mid 60's and early 70's. There is a tsunami of grey coming and they steamroll over everything — including death and dying.

When doing some research for this topic, I found out that the Benelux countries have MAID at 4.7% of all deaths. I sense that as more people discover it is available as an option, the more it will grow. When it comes to medically assisted deaths, cancer is by far (67%) the number one illness that people have.

For some people, the idea of deciding to be medically assisted in order to exit this world seems absolutely contrary to every fibre in their body. This book is not here to debate the merits of MAID. It is merely here to let you know that MAID is slowly becoming an option for some people. It is a difficult choice, but it is indeed a choice.

One of the things that has become more popular in the area of death and dying is the idea of hospice. Over the last decade, hospice has become more known and it has definitely helped families in a time of crisis. I truly believe that hospice provides a special bridge between what a family can offer and what a hospital can offer. I think it carefully blends the best of the serenity and quiet of home with the assurance that medical assistance is only a few meters down the hall.

I strongly believe that when you combine all the positive aspects of hospice care with MAID, you get a situation where the patient, the family and the medical staff can work together to find the most suitable path.

If and when you find yourself at a crossroads and you do not wish to continue living, it is absolutely vital that you have discussed your wishes. I'll readily admit, these are not easy conversations to have, but they are extremely important.

Grief

Grief. It's such a small word and yet it is truly mighty. Four letters have the power to absolutely destroy people and leave them shattered. I see grief daily at my work. I see it up close and very personal. This chapter is about grief and it's probably the most difficult one I've written. I am not going to regurgitate a whole bunch of stuff you can find on the internet about grief. Grief is a very personal thing and we all grieve in many different ways.

During a funeral, when a family requests an ID (identification) at the casket, we open up the back door of the coach so the family can see the deceased's face one last time. One of my coworkers will slowly move the casket forward and gently lift the lid. I will stand to the side and carefully open up an umbrella, ensuring the family has privacy. It is during these moments that I witness some of the most intense outpourings of grief.

Some people are stoic. They look at their dead relative or friend and keep a stiff upper lip. I am intimately aware of this type of grief. Born and raised for my first 7 years in Great Britain, the British are famous for their stiff upper lips and for keeping their emotions in check. Public displays of grief and affection are part of a society that is truly woven into my mind. I sense (and would hope) that things are a bit different almost five decades after my departure. But then again, there are many individuals who never wish to show their emotions in public.

The next type of person I see grieving is one that is experiencing what I would call profound grief. They are practically immobilized by grief. I have seen people finding it a challenge to put one foot in front of the other. Grief has hit them like a freight train. It has rocked them to their core, and they are frozen. They cry deeply and you can feel their pain.

In between the stiff upper lip and paralysis/wailing, you have a vast array of displays of grief. Kleenex tissues are clutched tight and gently dabbed onto faces. People stare despondently at the ground, never looking up. Still, others try a whole different tact and try to use humour to deal with the situation. I've come to believe that grief doesn't really care what you do — it just lingers there, ready to pounce and hit you.

At one particular funeral, I worked, a father had died due to a drug overdose. The ex-wife and three children came up to the casket crying. It was probably one of the most intense things I had ever seen. There wasn't just grief, there was a deep anger mixed with the grief. The children had written letters to their father which they placed into the casket. Now, with their father dead, there was no way he could read these words. I wonder how things might have turned out if they had managed to convey their thoughts to him before he died.

Of course, I will never really know the story of this man. It's all really conjecture at this point. Grief brings with it a lot of "should have, could have and would have" conversations. When we bury someone who has committed suicide or has died accidentally due to an overdose, there are two words that keep floating in my mind: "if only." "If only" is the precursor to "coulda/shoulda/woulda." For some, it offers a fleeting glimpse of explanation or a glimmer of hope. But this feeling gets pummeled by the reality of death. Grief is unrelenting and stealthy. It waits silently and slithers into people's brains at any moment.

When I witness grief flow through a crowd of mourners, I see how people try to support one another. Many wear sunglasses that they hope will deflect grief. In most cases, it's merely a prop. Their body language tells the whole story.

They shake with grief. As they try to console each other with hugs and heartfelt words, grief consumes the crowd.

Some people grieve for a relationship that might have been. We grieve knowing that there may have been countless opportunities to connect over the decades that were never taken. I call this type of grief, stealth grief. You think you're grieving for one thing, but in actual fact, you are grieving for something completely different.

Grief doesn't just apply to people who have died. It can apply to breakups, pets, missed opportunities and of course jobs. I have been fired a few times. It was painful, but I didn't really grieve. In at least one case, it was a relief to be let go. I was a terrible receptionist. In my defense, this was before voicemail was invented.

When I look back on the past year of publishing *Concrete Wave Magazine*, I realize that I was entering a period of grief. But the grief manifested itself that went beyond merely stealth grief. I had watched with alarm as my advertisers started to abandon the magazine for the digital shores. YouTube, Facebook and Instagram were starting to become a big deal. I felt powerless to stop things. I used to compare the change to a watercolour artist who was told one day to throw away his brushes, paint and canvas and pick up a hammer, chisel and a slab of marble. The artist in me was finding it incredibly difficult to master the new digital realm. I couldn't understand the financial model and ink had coursed through my veins for so long that I felt lost in pixels. I knew the magazine was in a death spiral, but I couldn't figure out a path forward.

Looking back, I realize now that I was paralyzed with fear of not really knowing what to do. I started to become unsure, and my creativity started to seize up. You can probably imagine what happened next. I started to get writer's block. I lost my mojo. The entire experience was isolating and deeply frustrating. This is the extraordinary power of grief. It will consume you and twist you in ways you never thought imaginable.

Despite this dark period, I did manage to navigate it. I gave the magazine to a fellow skater to see if he could carry on the message. It felt like a massive weight had been lifted from my shoulders. It took over three years for me to start writing again and get my mojo back.

There is no doubt that grief can destroy you if you let it. I think that I rode grief for the magazine a bit like a wave — and it ties in nicely with the title of this book. When you surf the waves of grief that hit you, you have to be very careful not to get overwhelmed by a close-out or pulled into the undertow. Grief is a cruel master. It forces you to confront reality. You can't outrun grief, but it is possible to grow from it.

Some Final Thoughts

The summer of 2023 represents 48 continuous years of me riding a skateboard. It also happens to be the first year that the Olympics will have skateboarding as an event. While there were hints of doing this back in skateboarding's first wave during the 1960s, it does seem a bit surreal to see it actually happening. Then again, having been through a number of waves in the popularity of skateboarding, the Olympics are not going to have any impact on my life. With respect to skateboarding, the only thing that has an impact on my life are the people who I have met and continue to meet because I am a skateboarder.

Earlier on in this book, I mentioned that 25 years ago I came up with the idea of calling my book on skateboarding's history "The Endless Wave." The publisher and I eventually decided to call it "The Concrete Wave." In some strange way, I feel like I've had the opportunity to have my cake and eat it too. But the last few years of the magazine were not easy. Getting writer's block was truly a diabolical experience. It really did feel like something in me had died. I still loved skateboarding, but I felt I had come to a crossroads in trying to figure out how to move forward.

After much soul-searching, I realized that it was time for me to change. There were many days of feeling like a deer caught in the headlights. I am glad I made the decision I made. It was necessary to cut my ties with the magazine and let others take the reins. Letting go is a part of dealing with loss.

When I first started writing this book, I was doing it alone. Through a podcast I created, I had the opportunity to meet up with Nathan Ho. Nathan has indeed lived up to his name. Not only did he motivate me to write, but his contribution has made this a much better book than if I'd done it alone. Even this is a new experience for me and having a collaborator feels pretty damn good.

I hope this book becomes a launching platform for you. Death encompasses so many different things including grief, active listening, legacy work and green burials. No matter where you wind up on your research, I hope that in some small way, this book has helped you start that journey.

From the start, I knew that pairing the subjects of death and dying with skateboarding would strike some as odd or bizarre. But speaking as a skater here, I really don't give a shit. If the subject of death is something you hadn't considered before, then this book has done its job. I am acutely aware that there is a high probability of someone taking the ideas found in this book and taking them to a much higher level. That's ok — the same thing happened when "The Concrete Wave" first hit. If there hadn't been my book, it's unlikely that Spin Magazine would have done a story on Dogtown and Z Boys and that documentary wouldn't have been made. It makes me think how many other amazing stories within skateboarding are still buried just waiting for the right exposure.

When I was growing up, I distinctly recall my mother quoting George Bernard Shaw's famous saying "Youth is wasted on the young." While I can understand where Shaw was coming from, I'd wish he'd lived long enough to try skateboarding. The funny thing about skateboarding is that if you stay with it long enough, you will wind up in a wonderful dual world of youthful adulthood. I never stopped doing something in my childhood/adolescence and it has carried me through life for almost 5 decades.

Back in the mid-90s, skateboarding looked very different than it does now. I'd like to think that in some small way, I helped to contribute to this change. But then again, the industry knew what it needed to do before I came along. Just have a peek at this article *https://dansworld.com/meeting.html*. Perhaps this book will inspire someone to write a piece that will bring about more changes to the way people view death.

On a final note, working in the deathcare does elicit some strange reactions. People wonder if I actually have to pick up a dead body. But strange reactions are nothing new to me. I had plenty of experience as a skater. Some people might think I'm a weirdo for still riding at my age. I get the occasional funny look or honk from the horn of an irate driver. But none of this can take away from the sheer joy and freedom I feel when I am out there skateboarding.

If you have enjoyed reading this book, feel free to contact me at *theendlesswavemichael@gmail.com*

Postscript
(The Future Is Unwritten)

When I first started to contemplate the idea of this book, I wasn't quite sure where it would lead to. There are literally thousands of books about death and dying. What I am really trying to do with this book is spark a conversation that may or may not have happened. After all, most people are uncomfortable talking about death and dying — and this includes skateboarders.

I see this book as a catalyst to kickstart these difficult, but very necessary conversations. It's pretty ironic — skaters often give off an air of fearlessness and a desire to push things past a limit. But when it comes to discussing death, they become remarkably quiet.

I am not looking here to do a bait and switch, either. I have tried to blend some of the stories that I've experienced as both a skater and a worker in the death care industry. I'd be the first to agree this blended subject is aimed at a pretty niche audience. But I also sense that it will resonate with those it's supposed to.

Every skater I've ever met remembers the first time they tried to skate. They remember getting pulled into the magic of the experience. Whatever the catalyst — a big brother, taking their sister's roller skates or just seeing someone skate down the street — they got a spark and it turned into a burning flame.

The ability to continue to enjoy skateboarding past your teenage/young adult years is something that very few people really get to experience. Despite skateboarding's incredible popularity, one glance at a local skatepark will tell you all you need to know — if you're lucky, you might spot one or two folks over the age of 30. The good news is that as skateboarding has expanded its vision, there are more older folks rolling on longboards.

If skateboarding was a catalyst that brought you into an entirely new world filled with unique experiences, then I hope that this book inspires you to plunge into finding out more about death and dying.

Take time to visit a death cafe. This is where people gather in a very informal setting to discuss death and dying. It can be done in a medium-sized group or online. Visit websites and learn about the myriad of services that are available. The more armed you are with information, the less likely you'll feel vulnerable. Funeral homes bank on this vulnerability. A little knowledge can make all the difference in the world.

While it can be hard to talk with your significant other, about death and dying, it can be extremely worthwhile. Explaining what you feel about quality vs quantity of life is just one thing you can discuss. Make sure your wishes are communicated now because there may come a time when you are incapacitated. No one will know what your wishes are and this will lead to a great deal of anxiety and frustration.

Death brings life full circle. Stephen Jenkinson writes about this extensively. Here is just one of his many quotes:

"The meanings of life aren't inherited. What is inherited is the mandate to make meanings of life by how we live. The endings of life give life's meanings a chance to show. The beginning of the end of our order, our way, is now in view. This isn't punishment, any more than dying is a punishment for being born."

The roots of my journey in the world of publishing started over 26 years ago. I can't wait to see where the next 26 years take me. But as Joe Strummer famously wrote, "the future is unwritten."

PART TWO

Taking Things to a Whole Other Level

By Nathan Ho

Inspiration For
The Endless Wave

From the moment I first stepped onto a skateboard, I knew that it was all that I ever wanted to do. There was just this inner-knowing and burning desire to learn how to skateboard. Through skateboarding, a part of me felt free to explore my surroundings and myself. I felt like I was able to appreciate and connect with my world. Skateboarding always appealed to me because there were no rules to follow and everybody was welcome.

In another light, I'd always felt different to the other kids growing up, like I was an alien from another planet. From as young as 3 years old, I can recall seeing colors, energies and spirits, having precognitive visions and actively leaving my body at night. I was a very quiet kid growing up, which I can attribute to a lot of processing of the different energies, emotions and thoughts passing through me. I had plenty of questions about life and the things that I was experiencing, but growing up in a religious family limited the availability of people who could accept and understand me. I also wasn't the most coordinated child (gosh these human bodies can be difficult to master), so this translated into fumbling and clumsy mistakes in everyday activities and other sports that added to feelings of being ostracized and criticized for my differences.

Despite all my differences, skateboarding gave me a place to feel at home in my body and mind. Throughout the years, I met some amazing friends and people who gave me the acceptance and encouragement that I craved. Skateboarding was our language and one that we learnt to speak together. Those who got to know me, let me know that it was okay to be myself.

While my spiritual experiences dwindled during my teenage years, they were still etched in my mind and a big mystery for me. Conversations about spiritual experiences were off limits to my family and friends outside of skateboarding, because I already felt actively judged on almost everything. Skateboarding was my pathway to self-discovery, and it was during my early 20's that my spiritual senses became active again.

The trust, diversity and acceptance amongst my inner circle of skateboarders is what inspired me to explore and learn more about my spiritual path. It was too loud to ignore and I couldn't just turn it off. I furthered my studies in metaphysical topics, developed my abilities with the guidance of a mentor, began my practice as a Clairvoyant Healer and began exploring the world from a renewed perspective.

As I learnt to accept and express myself on all levels; physical, mental, emotional and spiritual, I felt a huge shift in my appreciation, love of life and the people in it. Because I was free to express myself, I was able to experience parallels in the elation that I experienced through spirituality and skateboarding.

Outsiders of both skateboarding and spirituality are commonly misunderstood and judged. Spiritual seekers might be thought of as *"alternative, freaks, hippies or weirdos"*, while skateboarders might be perceived as *"rowdy, troublemaking punks"*. I know that both people involved in skateboarding or spirituality have a set image in mind of what each other looks like, which can often make the two paths seem very distant and different to one another.

I always felt like the two paths were very distinct, yet very similar. Skateboarders are like spiritual seekers or pilgrims and vice versa. The continual journey of continual self-improvement, seeking holy lands and sacred places immortalized in scriptures, skateboard magazines and videos, applying learnt skills to new situations, reflective practices, openness, flow, acceptance and compassion. Skateboarding is a practical and applied form of spirituality at its best!

So many similarities have revealed themselves to me in both paths and it has been through having a foot in each world, that I have been inspired to bridge both worlds. Although it has taken me several years to be able to articulate and be completely transparent about my experience of skateboarding and spirituality, the exact day that I asked for help from Archangel Michael *(a strong, supportive Angel who oversees things such as protection, life-path and important life-decisions)* and declared that I wanted to begin a new writing project, was the exact day that Michael Brooke, of *Concrete Wave Magazine*, contacted me about the first blog post that I wrote about Spirituality and Skateboarding. The post that I made on Spirituality and Skateboarding dated back to 8 years ago, reading on the calendar as the date of Michael's birthday!

All this in the space of one request of divine intervention was a strong indication that I was on the right path! Michael shared that since selling *Concrete Wave Magazine* he had been working as an assistant at a funeral home and also had several spiritual awakenings of his own in recent years. We exchanged our perspectives on several topics, which then led our conversations to be directed toward the possibility of writing a book together.

I feel safe and free from judgment being around skateboarders and spiritual people. In both worlds, although my friends were not always able to understand or relate to what I was talking about, they always listened without judgment. I felt like I've always wanted to write and share my ideas about my inner and outer worlds with others. I want to inspire the amazing people in skateboarding to be the very best they can be, in grounded, practical and relatable ways.

Freeing Skateboarders from the Fear of Death

Many of us have been taught to be scared when death shows its face. Death is in fact, an essential and a natural part of life. In order to overcome any fears that we have about death, we need to understand it and contextualize it through concepts that can help us to explore it.

It might be common to think of life and death as two ends of a linear experience, however, life and death are part of a cycle. There cannot be one without the other. New life and new beginnings are the result of an end and a conclusion to another. In this cycle and recycling of different things, whether it be life, experiences or opportunities, one cannot go through the process of life without the process of death.

We often think of death and dying as the end of the road. Some common questions and themes that I have come across are:
"Where to from here?
Does everything just stop?
Do we lose everything that we have accumulated?
Our possessions?
Our knowledge and abilities?
Our skills?
If we are all going to die anyway, why should we bother trying or why should we bother living?"

These questions come to the surface if we are to think of the life experience as linear. We are all here as souls in a physical body to grow, learn and unleash our own personal and wider-world expressions into the world. Thinking about the journey that we go through as a Soul and not just a Human is one of the most profound ways to understand that we are so much more than the current experiences of our bones, blood and flesh.

When we understand and realize that we are so much more than our humanness, we can then start to understand that as souls, we each have a journey. A journey from life to life, place to place, with a focus, intention, passion and purpose. With all due respect to religion, the concept of an afterlife can be used in some religions to scare or disempower people. However, in my experience of life, death and the other side, one thing to be assured of is that we all have an afterlife.

It's not a matter of elitism, where only certain individuals on certain paths make it. Some big questions around this are, *"is it place? Where is Heaven? What is Heaven?"*

In my experience, the afterlife is what we make of it. What we want our afterlife to be, we will live it. Connecting with those who have crossed over, I've been shown these beings in their happy place. They have the ability to live out their most memorable experiences in their lives. They are free from any pain or illness that they experienced before they departed. The deceased are able to freely travel between places and be with their family and friends who have also passed over. No one is alone unless they choose to be on the Other Side. It's like they've passed through an inter-dimensional veil. They are still here and with us but on a different frequency or bandwidth.

Life takes on a new form in the afterlife. Is the afterlife even the afterlife? What if this is life? What if our experiences here in the human form are experiences of pre-life?

Having understanding and knowledge of this frees us from anxieties about dying itself. Born and reborn again, we are able to live in more confident and enjoyable ways.

The Soul is like the essence of who we are. It is the being housed inside the vessel that we recognize and call the "Body". Living life in a Human Body is amazing, for it enables us the experience of being able to do many incredible things. Skateboarding is one of them. My Spirit Guide once told me that *"there is no other place in the galaxy that has something even remotely close to Skateboarding!"*

When we give something in our lives attention and focus, we are giving it energy and thus, we are giving it life. When we close off, disconnect or move on from something in our lives, we are in a state of closure, which does imply death. It is inherent in our nature to keep on expanding, growing and evolving. Think of the ways that we create, like a revolving door. One thing begins, and another ends.

Let's think of death as a phase. Just like how the moon has phases or the oceans have their high and low tides. In skateboarding, death can take on many forms and expressions of this cycle. Death might imply the end of one particular experience, at that specific moment in space and time and yes, there may be some fear of the unknown of what to expect afterwards, but rest assured, the times ahead lead you towards better and brighter things.

Usually, it's the fear of the unknown that holds us back. The fear of a form of death and dying translates to hanging on. It's these moments when we resist the transitions of these cycles, that we are faced with a range of emotions, such as anger, anxiety, depression, frustration and loss of direction. These emotions could contribute to being the catalyst for a range of experiences, such as injury, illness, isolation and mental health issues.

There are times when we know that the cycles of death and rebirth are present or they're coming. Life is taking place as you create in another direction! The expressions and experiences of life and death show up quite frequently in skateboarding. There may be times in skateboarding when you may feel that your focus is beginning to change and it's important to be able to recognize these changes and the kinds of actions to take.

Relationships with other skaters change and certain friendships grow stronger over the years, while others serve their purpose and they fade away. Perhaps you grow through your carefree years of youth into responsible adulthood together? Do you keep nurturing friendships that no longer feel right? Do you stay with friends who drain you energetically and emotionally?

Have you ever snapped your skateboard while trying a trick? Or broken a kingpin or popped your bearings while trying a trick? What about ripping a hole in your favourite pants while skating? Do you dwell on the fact that you need to part with your worn-out or broken product or do you make plans, take action and look forward to setting up a new board and doing it all over again right now or another time?

If you're the kind of skater who films your friends on video or you have your own tricks filmed, has your battery ever run out on you? What happens to the battery? It dies through its own sense of depletion and already, you're thinking about alternatives. Do you have a spare? Are you able to charge it? Let's get it sorted and try again.

If you're out skating by yourself, with friends, at a park or at a spot, the session itself has its own life and death. It's almost like the spot has a fire lit when this happens. The energy is amped up and it catapults you into another state of being. The process of warming up, having fun, enjoying the ride, resting, recovering and so forth. The session might end when tricks are landed, equipment is packed away, everyone is tired, the lights at the park go out or the neighbours complain and the security or police show up, but that never truly is the end. There is that feeling of moving on and looking forward to the next session — the rebirth.

Within the skateboard industry, product ranges, team riders and skateboarding itself change. New skateboard graphics, clothes and shoes are released each season. Team riders come and go throughout the years. These companies need to keep up with skateboarding and it's also been common for team riders to start their own companies, and form their own brands when their creative drive and vision expands beyond the teams that they are a part of. Or in other instances, some companies and brands die a death of their own and this drives the people involved through their own form of rebirth into different directions of interest.

When you are skateboarding, there is a chance that injuries may have the potential to push you into this transition where a part of you may die. Overcoming your fears is a part of this cycle of life, death and rebirth. What can you change so that you can handle this and adapt to it? Do you overcome your fears or do you let them get to you? Are there alternatives to what you're looking at doing on your skateboard?

In order to get closer to landing your trick, can you change the angle you approach, your speed, feet placement or weight distribution? Know that the very essence of trying and toying with the possibilities of your imagination are a form of giving life to your ideas. All creation starts on a mental level first before it can exist in the physical reality. For example, if you've given life to an idea of a trick at a spot, you can either continue to nurture it or your idea can die and be reborn in the form of perhaps a different trick or finding a different spot for it.

It's incredible how much creativity exists within skateboarding itself, for this is what will keep this activity, culture and lifestyle thriving for many years to come.

In my own journey on my skateboard, I started out in my teens learning to skate on the streets, to finding my way around transition and parks in adulthood and now to skating into the unknown in my mid-30s. In my own phases of life and death in skateboarding, I've gone through different phases and several knee injuries. I have lost my ability and confidence to skate stairs and gaps. Through muscle wear, I've lost my ability to pop my board high enough for a range of flip tricks and skating on ledges. It's been like farewelling long-time friends and it was frustrating to deal with initially.

If I had dwelt on the fact that my body had changed and I kept pushing to do the same calibre of tricks, I probably wouldn't be skating today, but through commitment and passion for skateboarding, I've been able to redirect my energy into skating less-orthodox spots and still have fun with it. In more recent years, I've become a parent and have two sons who have also shown an interest in skateboarding. The death of one part of me led to the birth of another part of me and it has been a great bonding experience for us.

When a part of us dies, a new part of us is reborn. The process of dying and rebirth acknowledges the fact that life can indeed, take on many forms. Dying and rebirth provide us with the opportunity to look at what we really value in life or within our context of creation. It provides us with the opportunity to really be present and enjoy what we are doing. Letting go of the fear of dying amplifies our ability to be present and engage with the present.

Dying does not simply mean the end. Rather it implies the beginning of the next. I believe in openly expressing to the universe, *"this or something better"*, meaning that whatever you are experiencing right now, is a reflection of your best or working towards your best suited offering of life right now. What feels right for you at this moment? What feels like it's your best expression right now?

There is always learning to be done. A true master is one who learns something and continues to expand on their practices. This might happen within skateboarding. For example, how many times have you practised that same line in the bowl or how many times have you kickflipped, only to find yourself searching for more? More spots, more obstacles, more ways to kickflip into, onto, over, up, down?

This might also happen outside of skateboarding, like in the form of *"what else can I learn?" "What life skills have I learnt from skateboarding?" "What pathways have opened up to me because of my involvement with skateboarding?"*

For me, my experience of death in skateboarding was about asking myself the question *"do I still want to be skateboarding? Does skateboarding still have life for me? Do I still have the life for skateboarding?"*

The bottom line is that a part of you can die while another one is reborn. There might be fear around the *"what's next?"*, but know that if the passion and love for something exists, there is the opportunity for it to live on and take another form.

Many skater-owned companies, skateboard artists, photographers and videographers are a great example of this. They may have had their time in the spotlight years ago and they left their legacy behind, paved the way and made their contribution to their respective world, then their love for skateboarding is what gave them another opportunity to rise from the ashes.

The journey of souls is like this too. We live our lives, make our impact, and leave our legacy, body and physical life behind. It's the love that exists between the worlds of the living and dearly departed that allows the veils to thin and worlds to coalesce. It's love that makes this possible in the afterlife through the arrangement of future soul contracts; presenting the opportunity to reincarnate around and within similar or the same soul groups and the guise of messages, signs and visitations from the spirit world.

In my experience of working with the spirit world, our ability to understand the concepts and experiences of reincarnation, the nature of soul contracts and communicating with a dearly departed family and friends is enhanced if both parties have had a strong flow of positive and loving emotions and memories exist between them. It's the openness to love that amplifies this connection between the worlds of the living and dearly departed.

Whether it be in skateboarding, life on earth or life in the afterlife, love unites the worlds of life and death and empowers one to be able to roll forever in whatever form life decides to take on.

Skateboarding and the Language of Love

What is it that skaters bond over? How does it happen? Why does it happen? Have you ever been to a new park, city or spot and felt the awkwardness of that first greeting to your fellow skateboarder? On the outside, it seems that even though you both enjoy doing the same thing, you're bound to get along right? You might then proceed to stand back and watch or they might watch you for a while, like you're getting a feel for each other and the new environment that you're in before potentially engaging in more conversation.

It doesn't matter what country or town you are in as this seems to be the way that it always goes. Whether the place you are in speaks your language or not, you can pick up on this vibe through the body language and looks that are coming your way. Sometimes you may feel those eyes looking at you as you are skating and finding your way around your surroundings.

It's like you are entering into someone else's territory and you need to show your respect before entering in full presence. What is really going on here, is an exchange of emotional energy in the form of love for skateboarding.

Those who show up to a spot with the intent to stir up the environment and vibe of existing skaters gathered there will not be well received or welcome. Those that show up and want to have fun without the expense of conflict, damage or disrespect to the spot and the people there. Simply put, if you show up and you're down to skate, then you'll most likely enjoy the experience immensely. If you show up and make a scene, tip over the trash, break bottles and other objects, climb on things, set the bins on fire or do anything that brings unnecessary attention to the park or spot, then it might be time to stop, pack your things and go.

This attention-seeking kind of behaviour is a communication of their own need for greater acceptance of self and self-love. This kind of off board behaviour reflects on seeking worthiness through being a clown, however, it reflects a poor image of Skateboarders and the way they behave in the environment that they are in.

As long as you show up and have clear intentions of having fun and follow the flow of what's going on there, you'll most likely be welcomed. Skateboarding has the potential to bring so many different worlds together. It might be similarly said about any other activity, hobby or spot, however, because skateboarding is so accessible in urban-style environments and there is not a specific place that people have to go in order to participate, the influence of Skateboarding has a profound impact on shaping culture, identity and lifestyle.

Skateboarding can open its doors to each and all who want to have a go. Skateboarding takes place in many different styles, breaking social constructs in the barriers of age, demographics, gender and socio-economics. Many bonds are formed over boards. It's safe to state that while there are certain skills a skateboarder has to learn in order to progress, every skateboarder is unique; learning and expressing in their own way. Most, if not all skaters can relate to similar journeys as they progress.

Skate for fun, enjoy the process and show up as the best version of yourself, on and off board. The tricks that you do are secondary to sharing and expressing the language of love while you are on your skateboard.

Different Styles, Different Smiles

The many different styles of skateboarding could be likened to the diverse options in religions that people can choose from. In religion and skateboarding, each has their own distinctive focus and features that set them apart.

Religion presents this through differences in lifestyle, beliefs, values, celebrations and rituals. Religions have an influence on their followers by encouraging them to engage in certain practices such as periods of fasting, prayer and worship and feature a calendar that influences their time dedicated to their path and everyday living.

The different styles of skateboarding can be defined through the different kinds of skateboards, tricks, terrain and places to skate and the type of skating that you enjoy will most certainly influence your lifestyle. Skateboarding doesn't have any rules as such, however the different styles of skating can definitely have an impact on how you plan out your time.

For instance, if you're into skating transitions and parks, you might head to the skatepark early in the morning at the crack of dawn or spend hours upon hours at the park or ramp. Or if you're a street skater, you might have certain spots that you can skate, like business and industrial districts and school yards outside of hours, on weekends and public holidays.

Irrespective of whatever path you choose in a faith or a type of skateboarding, one has their place of practise and the connection to the experiences and the expression. It turns out that subconsciously, in every skateboarder is a seeker and in every religious devotee, there is a seeker.

What could it be that these seekers are searching for? Could it be enlightenment? Enlightenment is not an end goal, but rather it is an ongoing process. Enlightenment of the body, mind and spirit and both paths have the potential to achieve both as participants of both religion and skateboarding ideally cultivate their experiences and work towards self-improvement, growth and appreciation of the world within them and around them.

At their best, religions can start as a place that people can turn to for some opportunities to find a sense of belonging, develop discipline, morals, friendships and participation in practices to help them make sense of themselves and the world. Skateboarding might look like another sport or physical activity, however, beyond this, there are also opportunities for similar things that religion offers, such as acceptance, belonging, discipline, friendship and understanding of self.

After becoming aware of what religion and skateboarding have to offer, one might be led to ask the question "which one is the best?", or "Which one is correct?", no one truly knows and no one can answer that question for anyone else except for themselves.

At times, people from different paths might be convinced that their way is the way and may display some bias towards their own path. They may argue about which is best or put down other paths or the people that follow them, in an attempt to influence others to join their cause. Representatives from one religion may promote their religion as the right one and the others are false representations of the divine. There might be skaters calling skaters of other genres "kooks" because of the popularity of one form of skating over the other.

When this happens, there is a disconnection from the essence or the roots of both religion and skateboarding. Sure they might look and feel different on the outside at an extrinsic level, however on an intrinsic level, the experience is very similar.

The different religions and styles of skateboarding could be likened to different species of trees. They are the same at their core but different in other ways. It could be said that without different representations through different species, how could there be growth or evolution on a bigger picture scale? The diversity in religion represents diversifying understanding of the world, often intertwined and growing out of the world's cultures, locations and experiences, while diversity in skateboarding represents a way of adaptation and growth in response to developments in hardware, experimenting with new terrain and pushing the boundaries in different environments.

Asking whether one is right or wrong is not the question, but more so, the question to ask is whether this one is right for you? Each has its own collective which underpins and influences its devotees, which leads them to connections to their own individualized expression. These expressions can then be likened to the sounds of musical notes singing their praises to the highest expression of love and creation. In religion, these musical notes are praises to the song of the Divine, via whichever path one chooses to explore this through. In skateboarding, the different styles are songs of praise to the spirit of skateboarding and a homage to the skateboarders of the past, present and future.

Skateboarding and The Soul

What is a Soul? Do we all have one? A soul isn't something that we have but rather, it's something that we are. We are spiritual beings having human experiences and the soul is that part of us that makes us experience being alive.

Consider for a moment, the body that you have. It's a human body. On its own, a body is a body on its own, a vessel for the soul that animates the body and brings it to life. Think of the body like a skateboard. On its own, the skateboard is just a skateboard and when someone rides it, the skateboard and the person come together and there is a bridged experience of rolling on the surface of the street, park, ditch or what have you.

Now that we have described what a soul is, many of us are probably wondering, "What does it mean to be a soul? Why does this even matter?"

When we acknowledge that we are spiritual beings and not simply human beings, we broaden the perspective of our life experiences. We can begin to understand that there are things that are much bigger and more powerful than what we know, that our experiences are all connected and there is a kind of spark that brings different forms of life together. We celebrate creation and our own personal growth and development. We are granted the opportunity to see life and death as necessary parts of our journey.

Through taking on and reclaiming your own spiritual identity, you can begin to understand that your experience of life goes beyond what you experience as a human in your body. The understanding and acknowledgement of the spiritual experience in the human form leads one to constantly challenge their understanding of their own identity and what is truly important and relevant for them. It's a journey of discovery that one has to embark on for themselves and it is not something that another person can do for them.

Someone might be able to preach to you about or sell you a 'spiritual experience' that is designed for a human, which has the look and feel of something beyond the ordinary, everyday life. These are the kinds of external influences that might have you feeling an altered emotional or physiological state and then its effects wear off afterwards, leaving you seeking more, but missing out on the authentic and true connection to your identity from within.

I'm certain in skateboarding, there are similar things that exist that challenge one's perception of identity and ability. These could exist in the form of products promising enhanced performance, companies that promise and compromise their riders, the rise of internet-famed skateboarders and the number skaters comparing themselves and intentionally trying to outdo each other and the infallible, celebrity-status of some skateboarders. Someone or something trying to get in touch with one's identity in an influential way, as an agent of promising change and connection of sorts on the outside, surface level but doesn't acknowledge or change anything on the inside.

In order to understand and appreciate our own soul, we need to strip it back to basics. What is important for us? What inspires us? What gives our life meaning? Looking at what feeds our soul, we are put in a position of living the life that fills us up from the inside out. It's also natural for this soul nourishment to change from time to time, to reflect upon the very things that delight, inspire and nurture us.

Ask yourself why. What is your intention behind what you are doing? If you can answer this question and feel like it is an expression of you and it brings you joy, then that is something that feeds your soul. That is something that you could consider a spiritual experience and growth for your soul. These answers might look different for everyone, yet on a deep and profound level, this level of questioning for yourself encourages you to look deeper within yourself and continue on that journey of self-discovery and self-actualisation.

In life, it's quite natural and healthy to take a reality check when you enter and transition from different life phases. What are your relationships with others like? Why are you in your chosen job? What or who inspires you? Are you having fun doing what you are doing? Dig deep. What is it about these people, places, things and situations that light a candle in your life and guide you towards finding and paving your own path? What connects you with others and empowers you to unconditionally accept and love others? What fills you up on the inside and makes you feel a sense of appreciation for living to be the very best person you can be?

On your skateboard, you might like to ask yourself why you do certain tricks, or ride in a certain way or on specific terrain. Are you doing this for yourself? Are you connecting with others and feeling inspired as you are inspiring? Are you choosing to express yourself freely, knowing that you can show up as the best version of yourself?

I know the value of having role models and having someone to look up to and it's important to consider that you're drawing inspiration from them and translating it into your very own unique form of expression. Role models in Skateboarding aren't those that we are trying to copy and emulate, but rather interpret and reformulate in our own way.

So what if you've been skating for x amount of years and you can't do the same tricks as your friends? So what if you have tricks that you can't do well? Who cares if others have comments to say about the way that you skate or what you wear? There are so many different ways that you can enjoy interacting with your Skateboard. Find what works for you and make that yours, you'll feel a lot better for it in the long run than having to deal with the impacts on potential anxiety, self-esteem and stress.

This relationship between the soul and the human body could be likened to the metaphor of the skater and the skateboard. A soul needs a body to experience the full spectrum of the human living experience, just as a skateboarder needs a skateboard to ride and interact with the world from their perspective.

The two need each other in order to express what is unique and individual about them. Although the lifespan of a skateboard is much shorter than a human body, the concept of the skateboard as a body helps to reiterate that there is a bond, presence and synergy between both in both of these instances.

It's true that a soul can exist in a body, but without feeling aware, engaged or present in it will lack the substance of an enriching life experience. The same goes for a skateboarder without these same things and this will be reflected in the outward appearance of their skateboarding — their attitude towards themselves and others, their approach to skateboarding and their style.

To be a soul in a body is to be alive. To be a skater on a skateboard is to be alive. To be a soul in a human body is to show up the very best way possible. To be a skateboarder with a soul is to skate to show up and be your best, not to be the best.

"The Key to Immortality is to Live a Life Worth Living"

The above beautiful quote is from the late Bruce Lee, whose image and philosophy have inspired many generations and been represented in several skateboard graphics and products over the years.

Through living a life where you give everything you've got, you have the potential to make a lasting impact that continues to live on in the spirit of others. What is it that you consider as your legacy? Is it something that is left behind at the end of your life or is it something that you can consciously leave behind each day?

Each day could be seen as a beginning and an ending, just like the nature of life and death. What is it that makes you wake up each morning? The alarm clock? Do you need to go to work? To get something to eat? Instead of thinking of the moment you wake up as just another day in your routine, wake up because you are waking up with passion and purpose.

Skate or die!!!

I'm sure many of you can relate to this one and I know the feeling of waking up, being excited to go skateboarding. Driven by my love for skateboarding, I'd wake up early, do what I needed to do quickly and efficiently, fuelled by the thought of going skating. In my younger years, I loved being with my friends, finding new spots and filming at different locations. It never bothered me how far we actually travelled to get to some of these places to skate. The thought and the thrill of sharing in the spirit of something that we loved so much was enough to kick start my day. In my parenting years, I have been enjoying going out skating either by myself or with my sons early in the morning before any pedestrians, traffic or security. I thought that there was something very special about having a park or a spot all to ourselves, like the feeling of being alone or with family, participating in something very special and sacred.

What are some of the ways that you can carry this *"skate or die"* mentality outside of skateboarding? Skateboarding grows on you and can have a deep impact on your lifestyle and sometimes it can feel all-consuming when we live and breathe it.

I find it particularly easy to lose sight of "skate or die" when injuries or setbacks take place. That feeling of trying something on your skateboard and ending up with a rolled ankle, hot pocket or heel bruise can make you feel like you don't want to do anything at all except skate again. To conquer what seemingly conquered you.

Some people may feel like they're going through a void in these circumstances and feel like they're just waiting around to go skating again. Everyone handles things differently based on where they are at in life. I've seen this take on the form of excessive drinking and lazing about in a lot of skaters. For some, it might take on the form of seeking out methods and modalities that will benefit their health and healing process. For me, I know that my injuries meant continuing to go out on sessions and getting more into filming and video making. Finding a new purpose and passion kept my fire burning.

How do we find purpose and passion in the world outside of skateboarding? Think consciously about what you're doing and who you are sharing life with. Consider this your everyday legacy; making memories that will last a lifetime. Think of your legacy like threads in a piece of fabric that are all interwoven together. It's not only key events or favourite past times that make your legacy, it's everything in between as well.

My angels and guides tell me that there is no such thing as a boring person, or a boring situation or a day to be bored. There are so many different ways that you can experience and enjoy your day. Each person has their own story, and there is no way that you could understand your life or another person's just with one glance.

We experience life through metaphorical lenses. On the days that you are able to go skateboarding, you experience passion and purpose through these lenses. Mentally tell yourself when you are going through this exchange of perspectives so that your days off board can still be purposeful and passionate.

Perhaps there is a kid at your skatepark who could benefit from a few pointers. Maybe your local skate shop has a community project or event that you can help out with? Your friends might appreciate someone who can film or take photos or you could learn to use video editing software. You can still be involved, it just takes on a different form and expression. What is it that can give your life meaning when you are required to see through different lenses? Consider what you have available to you in your surroundings that bless you each moment.

"Live in the now and be in the present". It's been said time and time again to the point that it's become a cliched kind of phrase, but what does it all actually mean? My Angels and Guides say that people who are anxious are too focussed on the future and depressed people are too focussed on the past.

For instance, when you are out skating, let's say you get kicked out of a spot. You may have been trying a trick there and you weren't victorious. Do you fixate on it and do you finish skating for the day? Moving on to the next spot, in order to have fun, do you concentrate on spots that are next on your list or do you focus on where you are right now?

What fun would you be having if you were hung up on every spot that you were kicked out of or skimmed over every spot that you visited and didn't spend any time considering the different angles and lines that you could be approaching from? I'm sure your crew wouldn't be keen on putting up with that kind of complaining either. Think about whether you are having fun and what you can change in order to get there? Who is with you? Are you in good company today? Is there anything that you can practise or anything new that you can try today?

When I have connected with clients' loved ones on the Other Side, it's common for me to hear about their regrets and sometimes unfinished business. They tell me about the things that they wished they had done and the things that they wished they had said. No one ever tells me about their wish to be lazier or bored.

This experience alone inspires me and my clients to live with passion and purpose! Even though our souls go through a journey and we are able to go from one life to the next, the truth is, we'll never experience this same life again. Not even a day or moment in time goes by where everything is identical to another.

Life is about living. Worrying and complaining, wallowing in doubt and things that weigh you down actually affirm and give power to the undesirable experiences that you actually don't want in your life. Rather than speaking about what you should be doing, (which has negative undertones that what you're currently doing is not good enough and projects your thoughts out into the future to another day, another moment), try consider speaking about yourself in the now, with statements beginning with "*I can*" and "*I am*". Speak about yourself as if you've already attained what you are seeking.

Think about what you can look back on as your days pass. Did you fill your days with joy? Or did you find your life boring and uninspiring? You have the choice and you have the power to change this!

I find that an attitude of gratitude is one that can help you reach these deeper forms of appreciation and value in creating an everyday legacy. Enjoy every push, pop and kickturn. Ride your skateboard like you mean it. It's an expression of love for the board you stand on and the wheels you roll on.

Connect with your dreams and the things that make your heart sing. Connect with the people around you who uplift your life experience and make you feel like you want to live a life worth living. Connect with yourself and all of the inspiring qualities that make you who you are.

Your experience here on earth, certainly is a unique one. My angels and guides have told me that there is *"no place in the entire Universe which is similar or like this planet and physical realm".* I've said it before and I'll say it again, they have also told me that, *"skateboarding is a one of a kind activity that doesn't exist anywhere else in the entire Universe."*

No matter where you are, who you are with, or what you are doing, enjoy it and live it out as a beautiful gift that is celebrated in every moment of your involvement, interaction, and intention.

The Halfpipe of Grief

What is grief? As an emotion, it is commonly experienced during a time of loss. It's common to associate grief with what we have come to know as death and it is the kind of emotion that can affect people in many different ways. Usually those experiencing grief find their way to process the range of emotions that can be felt during this time and those observing the grieving tend to watch from afar and be unsure of what to say or do. It's a very personal experience that requires something different, yet something similar.

While we have already explored the nature of the Soul and the Body and life after death, grief affects all of us, there's no denying about that. It doesn't matter how spiritual you consider yourself to be. It's part of our Human nature to explore and express our full range of emotions, grief included. Something that we are collectively learning to do, is learn to support each other and express grief in healthy ways and perhaps the way to do this, is to understand that grief has different stages and requires something different at each time.

For me personally, it's through skateboarding and its connections to a diverse range of people that I've experienced, felt and observed the most instances of death, dying and grief so I'd like to explore grief itself through the metaphor of skating a halfpipe.

When someone crosses over and is no longer with you physically, that is like learning to skate a halfpipe. It feels so foreign and new and could be likened to different stages of grief, which each have their own timing and are experienced differently for everyone.

Here are the stages as follows:

1. **Finding the ramp** — Have you found the ramp? Are you skating the rest of the park and noticing this one or avoiding it deliberately? Have you climbed up to the deck of the ramp to check out your surroundings?

Some people deny or can't believe that their loved one has departed. If you try to ignore the situation during the initial stages of grief you'd miss out on what awaits, leaving you stuck in your mind and emotions. Similarly if you deny the existence of the ramp itself, you may miss out on skating a fun form of terrain.

2. **Making preparations** — Does your skateboard need checking? Does the ramp need sweeping? You might like to put on a helmet and pads when you are learning to skate a halfpipe, just like how you might like to identify who is around you and can support you through the grieving process.

Just as you would seek out friends that you can share the session with and will encourage, empower and inspire you when you are skateboarding, you'd want to consider others who have experienced grief and can offer you the kind of support that you need.

3. **Taking the First Steps** — When you climb up the ramp and put the tail of your skateboard on the coping, maybe your knees are shaking, you're unsure of where to position your body weight and noticing that you're a number of feet off the ground. The mind starts to wonder, just like when you have a loved one crossed over.

In both instances, you may be asking yourself questions like, *"Am I doing this right? Is my foot on the board? Will I make it? What will life be like without this person in my life? Will they be alright? Will they be happy and free of pain or will they be living out their afterlife in pain and sadness?"*

As you're up there, you might have checked your surroundings, asked yourself more questions, maybe picked up your board and taken it off the coping to pull yourself together, and psych yourself up.

In the days of learning to skate a halfpipe, maybe you had to have these psyche up moments to motivate you and give you the push you needed to get up there, even just to put the tail of your board onto the coping. The first few days may have passed since losing someone. You might begin to recognize that the one you loved is not around.

4. Taking the plunge — The front foot goes onto the front deck bolts of your skateboard. You're about to take the plunge down. It's a foreign feeling to go through the motions of standing up, putting weight on the back leg, compressing the body and bending the front knee and taking that plunge in. Some of us change our minds, jump off at the last second and end up running down the transition or sliding down the ramp.

Some of us fall on our first-ever drop-in attempts, maybe leaning too far back or forward and some of us ride it out to the bottom. If you do fall off your skateboard, do you get back up again and try again? If you hurt yourself, that's okay, take the time to recover and try again when you are ready. If you are observing someone try this for the first time, what do you do? Do you encourage them? See if they are alright?

Similarly in the early stages of acknowledging your grief and loss, you may have days when you feel the weight of your emotions coming down, like you miss your dearly departed loved ones. Go with the flow of your emotions. It's okay to cry if you need to, just like how it's okay to take your tail off the coping if you need a moment to pull yourself together. Check-in with your friends who you see needing that extra support.

5. The next transition — If you stay on your skateboard after dropping in, you'll soon be riding through the flat and approaching the next transition. What do you do to get to the top of the next transition? Do you stay as you are with your knees bent and ride up and back down fakie? Do you kick turn? Do you pump? You'll most likely end up losing your speed without pumping if you roll up and down, going from forwards and fakie or ride the ramp with back-to-back kickturns. To keep your skating thriving on this halfpipe, you will need to be present and you will most likely want to set your intentions on reaching the top of the transition to skate the coping.

Once you've dropped in on grief, you will have experienced acknowledgement and acceptance of the dearly departed. As you roll up forwards and fakie between the transitions of good and bad days and kickturn from ramp to ramp telling yourself to be strong, thinking you're fine, eventually you'll need to find ways to continue to live and thrive emotionally without the presence of your dearly departed. In the process of grief, you'll need to set your intentions to thrive by pumping through the transitions and skating the coping.

What is it that keeps you thriving in life once our loved ones have crossed over? Our Dearly Departed don't want us to be stuck and hung up on their absence. From their vantage point on the Other Side, they are the happiest when they can see us continuing to thrive in life. A part of them still lives on within and through our Hearts and memories.

6. Skating the Coping — Once you've dropped in and you start to pump to build up your speed, you'll reach the coping. You can hit the coping in many ways, maybe say, through stalling on the deck, grinding through the coping, doing an air or an invert. You are free to do whatever way you wish to express while you are up there, riding in your own way. Go up, do your thing and come back down, ready to keep up the flow and hit the next transition. There'll be times where you might only do one trick or many tricks at the top of the ramp on the coping, but whatever you do up there, I'm sure you can relate to the feeling and the stoke of skating in this kind of way as you go from transition to transition. With these actions, you are required to be present and engaged.

With the process of grief, the coping extends beyond literal *"coping methods"*. Coping methods can become a form of escape from the real emotions experienced as they encourage the body to become distracted and associate someone or something with handling an unpleasant emotion. Common practices in processing grief encourage the bereaved to find something to do that distracts them, to keep them from thinking about their loved ones. For some, they might focus on work, thereby working longer hours, while others may turn to alcohol or other substances so they can forget about their perceived loss.

Building upon the discussions that we have been sharing about life and the Afterlife, the passing of a loved one is not the end of their existence or their relationship with you. Your air at the other side of the transition, your grind, slide, stall or invert on the coping of grief takes on form through the ways that you cultivate, experience and express the continued relationship that you have with the dearly departed in order to celebrate and preserve their existence.

Some of the ways that you could skate this coping and keep your relationship thriving include:
- Celebrating their special occasions that were meaningful for them such as birthdays,
- Carrying out a community project in dedication to the dearly departed,
- Connecting through dreams by looking at a photo of them and asking them for a visitation before you go to sleep (when you are ready for it),
- Editing together their photos and memorable videos to share with others,
- Keeping belongings that had significant importance to them,
- Listening to their favourite music and songs that remind you of them,
- Recognising the messages and signs that they are communicating to you from the other side,
- Setting aside quiet time to talk to them in your Mind and
- Visiting places that were meaningful for them.

One of the most beautiful beyond worlds' friendships that I have witnessed grow over the years was between two best friends. He kept his best friend's skateboard and dedicated one day a year of skating on this skateboard at the very spot where they first met and grew up skating together. He also took this skateboard with him to skate at Love Park, Philadelphia, which was a very monumental street skating spot that these two best friends used to dream of going to together.

You'll find that the more that you participate in skating this metaphorical halfpipe of grief, you'll build up your momentum and flow and your connection to your loved ones on the other side grows. There are times when you'll really ease into the flow between your experiences with the Other Side and other times when you'll find difficulty in doing so. Allow this to unfold gently and at your own pace and know that through your own experience of this, you'll find inspiration and joy for living out life in honour of yourself and your loved ones.

Death and the departure of a loved one can happen so suddenly. It affects us all differently because every person in the physical side and on the other side is different. Each person that crosses over is like their own halfpipe. Different curves, sizes and styles of build make it different to skate.

The closer you are to the person, the bigger the halfpipe. Their departure will most likely affect you more than it does with someone who you may not have been as close to. There is a bigger learning curve, a steeper transition and maybe a scarier feeling of riding a bigger transition with a higher impact on your life moving forward. Despite all this, there is a deep sense of satisfaction that comes with learning to skate bigger transitions and the same goes for life and life after. While there are more impacting characteristics associated with losing someone closer to you, there will be a much stronger, more valid continuing relationship with them from where they are on the other side.

Take your time to process your grief as you would take time to learn to adapt to new terrain. It might feel uncomfortable at first and with your intention, dedication and participation, you'll find your own unique way to ride it out and keep the stoke going.

Love unites and binds through and beyond time and space. Each session, each ramp is different, yet so satisfying. The same can be said about each relationship that you have with those in your life, past, present and future.

Love to live and live to love. Skate or die!

The Third-Eye of Skateboarders

Typically, everyone has two physical Eyes that they can use to view the world in its physical form. Basically, the eyes function by receiving light, which sends a message to the brain and translates it into an image for us to see. We see the world around us that is made of dense matter, the things that we can see and touch with our Hands and interact with. There are things that we cannot see with our Eyes, such as electricity, oxygen, sound waves and thought forms yet we acknowledge their presence because of the impact and relevance that they have in our daily lives.

What some of us may have learnt through the worldwide increase in availability and exposure to eastern practices such as Chinese Medicine, Reiki, Yoga, is that we also have a Third-Eye for viewing the world beyond its physical form. The third-eye is a part of our spiritual anatomy and it is located on our forehead, in the space between our eyebrows. Physiologically this is known as the Pineal Gland, (which is responsible for bodily functions such as hormone production, growth and production of melatonin, which regulates sleep levels) and the name '*Third-Eye*' comes from its location and functions based on sensitivity to light.

The Third-Eye can allow us to see things such as energy, colored lights, dreams with clarity and visions of the past, present and future. The Third-Eye is typically developed through meditation and different forms of energy healing.

Activities that relax the body and mind and help to generate feel-good chemicals such as Dopamine, Oxytocin and Serotonin, support the flow and production of Melatonin. Anything that supports the function of your Pineal Gland and keeps it actively engaged can thereby support the operation of your Third-Eye and the added depth to your perception of the world. Regularly circulating these feel-good Brain chemicals throughout your body also helps to prolong the aging process!

While being able to see through the Third-Eye is considered the holy grail of many people on the path of spiritual development practices, what really needs to emphasized is that the Third-Eye teaches us to see our inner and outer worlds through eyes of love and compassion and also develops as a result of doing what you love, loving what you do and being with the ones you love.

These kinds of activities help you to engage in and experience seeing through your Third-Eye. You might be seeing through this part of you already without realizing that your Third-Eye is in operation, like the times when you dream about your loved ones, see creative opportunities in work, play and pleasure and naturally perceive the finer details about things that you are actively involved in.

Skateboarders have a unique ability to see the world differently as if they have an extra Eye allowing them to see beyond everything that exists before them. Skateboarding is a very immersive, one of a kind activity that is very accessible and can be done almost anywhere with almost anyone who shares the same passion and ideals as you.

Outside of skateboarding, people can be quick to form judgments about others based upon the different conditions that influence their living and lifestyle, such as age, employment, recreational interests, socio-economic status, sexuality and overall life experience. Think for a moment — if it wasn't for skateboarding, would you have met the kinds of people that you know?

The love of Skateboarding brings people together. Skateboarders that are out there skating for the love of it develop an ability to see beyond these different life-variables. Resulting from Skateboarding's accessibility is the potential to build relationships with people from very different and diverse backgrounds. I know many people have been able to find a sense of belonging, friendship and family through skateboarding.

People typically see the urban environment in a very what-you-see-is-what-you-get, purpose-built kind of way. A bench is for sitting on, a sidewalk is for walking on, a curb is to separate the road from the sidewalk, stairs and handrail are for going up and down and a pool is for swimming in. I'm sure you can relate to the experience of being kicked out of a spot for skating, like the neighbour, hero or authority figure that doesn't understand Skateboarding, with comments like, *"What are you doing here? Why are you skating here? This isn't a skatepark! You've got everything you need there!"*

The love for skateboarding opens one up to see these different parts of the environment in very different ways. Through the Eyes of a skateboarder, the world is a playground. That empty pool becomes the next session for a group of friends. That bump in the sidewalk becomes a booster to put a trash can next to so it can be Ollied over. That bench becomes an object to grind and slide on. The stairs that people walk down can be skated up or down.

Without skateboarding, would you have visited or traveled to the places that you have been? People that don't get skateboarding may look on and think that this is vandalism, while skateboarders look for opportunities and avenues to express their craft and spread their energy.

There are many areas within the urban environment that often seem like they're neglected and unused or utilized in ordinary and mundane kinds of ways, like say, the abandoned building, empty car park, ditch on the side of the road, set of stairs around the back of a building, loading dock that gets used once a week for deliveries or the benches in the plaza that only few people walk through during the working week. By day, these places are colourless and dull from barely anyone stopping to appreciate and marvel at and outside and beyond of this, skateboarders roll in with a fresh, loving perspective and light up the spots with their love, creativity and playfulness.

It's a known fact that people don't usually feel safe in quiet areas that are lifeless and seem abandoned. People typically avoid these places because they think that trouble lurks in these areas. Skateboarders see these places with love and they bring life and activity to these areas. There is the potential for pedestrians to stop and watch skateboarders and with this increased activity also bring in prosperity to the environment and the surrounding businesses and shops.

I know it can be frustrating to see new urban developments with purpose-built skate-stopping devices and saddening to see changes to current skater frequented environments to prevent further skateboarding from taking place. The truth is, that love always wins. Love always conquers fear. As long as there are streets to roll on, skateboarders will always be able to see opportunities which allow skateboarding to continue to thrive and live on through the people that love and cherish it so much.

There is a greater purpose for skateboarders in the urban landscape.

The Third-Eye of skateboarders empowers and enables them to see the world in ways that others usually can't. They connect to the vibration of love and send it into the ground, sharing it everywhere that they roll.

Skateboarders and Suicide

Before we go any further, I do acknowledge that suicide is a sensitive topic that can have a large impact on those close to the person that has taken their own life. Through this topic, I would like to debunk some of the myths around suicide and explore it through the metaphor of focussing your skateboard; when one deliberately and continually stomps in the middle of the skateboard to break it.

Suicide takes place over a drawn out process and is the end of the line for someone who has been experiencing a range of overwhelming and stressful emotions towards their life over a prolonged period of time. Usually a suicide takes place when the person has had these kinds of overwhelming emotional experiences built up without healthy ways to address and process these and they feel like they can no longer cope with the conditions that they are facing in their lives. It is an escape from these experiences with the intention of not coming back. It's an exit from their present state of experiencing life.

Focussing a skateboard has its parallels. Perhaps you may have focussed your skateboard during times when you felt like skating was not working out for you, you were feeling the frustration of not landing a trick at a spot, you had an injury, like your board hitting a previously cut up wound on your Shins. However you may have experienced this and the deliberate end to the lifespan of your skateboard, I'm going to assume that there was a build up and a desire to release the accumulated emotion and stress caused by some of these factors. Your foot goes through your skateboard, eventually it cracks, then snap! Your foot has gone through the middle of the board and it has divided into two, with the middle of the board touching the ground. Session over today! This skateboard is not coming back!

I know what it's like to lose people that I've cared about through suicide. I know it impacts on friends and family pretty heavily. There are a lot of questions around "why" and a lot of anger and sadness directed towards the suicide victim. It's understandable that there are going to be these emotions. The person has taken their life, most likely left without saying goodbye and they aren't coming back (physically).

The same thing happens when a skateboard is focussed. If you're out on a session and someone has focussed their board, it impacts on the mood and the energy of everyone. There are times where a focussed skateboard kills the vibe of the session for everyone. Unless they're carrying a spare board with them, they're not going home with their skateboard today. They'd probably be walking to the next spot, driving home or sitting around for the remainder of the day.

When someone has been experiencing prolonged stress caused by various conditions in their life, it has impacts on their physical, mental and emotional health. It is going to accumulate without a way to process this or release this. Sometimes there may be some early warning signs for individuals who have been going through the intensity of this kind of stress and other times it will feel like it has come out of nowhere.

The warning signs for someone being frustrated with their skateboard is very easy to identify. Perhaps there is more board throwing, negative self-talk, displays of anger and frustration and then there is the final straw that makes the foot go through the board. Thinking outside of skateboarding, what are some of the ways that you can identify when you or others are not operating at an optimal, emotional best? Pay attention to your own and others' behaviours and actions and notice any changes in their personality, attitude and overall demeanour.

How does one navigate this if there is no real way of telling what a friend or family member is thinking and feeling? Or if they haven't opened up to talking to you about these kinds of things? If you have been experiencing this level of overwhelm yourself, what are some of your own warning signs and outlets? You might need to pay more attention to these so that you can be emotionally available to help yourself and others when these changes take place.

Skateboarding through its health benefits and release of feel-good brain chemicals, can be a great physical outlet for releasing stress. Emotions that require processing require deeper connections to one's self and to others. Through the potentially diverse and enriching connections made through skateboarding, people can start to have more conversations, check in with and reach out to one another.

Whether someone has been contemplating suicide or focusing their skateboard, it's sad to say that the final choice is up to the individual involved. Though we can be instrumental in supporting them through processing and releasing their stressful and overwhelming situations, ultimately the end result does not sit with us. I know that if someone follows through with either of the two acts, it's common for a close friend or family trying to work with the suicide victim to take the blame and feel very responsible for what has happened, despite their best efforts to steer them in the other direction. Typically, there are questions raised and comments made, *"I could have done something", "it's all my fault, I'm the reason they're gone", "I wish I had reached out to them earlier."*

Despite the circumstances, I do know that any effort is better than no effort and though someone following through may not express it, your efforts are greatly appreciated to the victim and their family and friends. The convincing and counselling efforts are a reminder that someone does care for them.

There is a lot of judgement around suicide, just as there is with someone focussing their skateboard to end the session in frustration. The biggest emotion that I have observed to follow both of these acts is regret.

There are two paths that exist for a skater that has focussed their skateboard. They can be stuck in the past, being angry and frustrated at themselves for not landing their trick or for having a bad day on their skateboard. Moping around, dragging the vibe of the session down and being annoyed for the day. Or there is the reflective path that looks forwards, and they reflect on the possibilities that could have been if their board wasn't deliberately broken, like *"what if I took a break and gave this trick a few more tries?", "what if I calmed myself down, reflected on the experience of trying and tried a different approach next time?".* A skateboard can be easily replaced by going to the local skate shop and choosing a new board from the shelf and it doesn't take much to be back in action again.

In between the regrets of their choices, the words said and not said, the things done and not done, suicide victims are looking for a way out and somewhere to leave the situation that they are in. Suicide is typically deemed as the less forgiving, less desirable path because of the loss of life, the impact that it leaves on family and friends and the religious-influenced perspective towards it of someone going to Hell or living out their days in a punishing environment. From what I have seen in suicide victims when they've appeared to me, they're usually filled with sadness, grief and regret. Only once they've left, have they realised what and who they leave behind and have an impact on.

At times, they don't know that they've died, like they can't believe that they actually followed through with the act and are caught between the world of the living and the next.

Sometimes, they are living out a looped experience of their pain and hurts. This is the Hell that they put themselves through. They're not going to burn for an eternity however, as there is the opportunity for redemption once they become aware of their passing, go to the light and cross over to the other side.

All suicide victims go through a similar process to any other kind of death experience. Once they cross over, they have the opportunity to reflect on their life experience, observe the world from their new perspective, watch over their loved ones and choose another experience on earth at a later time, if they desire.

Deliberately ending the life of a human or a skateboard is never the desired option, but it does happen. Show your family and friends how much they mean to you. Let them know how much you appreciate them. Do things that fill up their emotional reserves and let them know how much they mean to you. Appreciate your life and progress in skateboarding and know how far you've actually come to get to where you are today.

Suicide or focussing a skateboard is never something to encourage another person to do, because when we find a passion and love for life, we want to make sure that we share the experience with others. When we are having a good time in life or out skating with friends and family, we want to share that experience of the energy that builds up and culminates in that environment.

While a human body isn't as easily or quickly renewed as a skateboard from the skate shop, it's safe to say that in skateboarding and in life, each individual creates their own version of heaven or hell while they are living on earth and with conscious awareness of the power and influence that they have with their life, what they choose to do with their life after this one is also their choice. Everyone is capable of living out a life filled with love and joy, it's a matter of the situations and environments that they surround themselves in.

Be part of the reason that someone wants to be alive and can be themselves.

Be the love that binds life between life, on board and off board.

Skating for Passion and Purpose

There are times in our lives where we may ask some of life's big questions, like *"why am I here?", "what's my purpose in life?",* or *"what's the meaning of life?".* The quest for meaning and purpose behind life and existence itself isn't so clearly defined and it is something that we all seek out to discover. We are by nature, expansive beings seeking to constantly evolve, so it isn't a matter of something to attain or achieve and all aspirations are finished, but rather it is a continual process that keeps on progressing and growing.

If we were not interested in expanding our experience and personal growth, we would happily settle to remain in the one fixed position. However, we learn, adapt, grow and change. It is the culmination of the passion and purpose, finding meaning in and connecting to what we do, that drives us to continue to want to live and learn more. Like in skateboarding. I'm sure that everyone can relate to the very first time that they stepped on their skateboard. Learning to stand on the board was a challenge in itself. Gradually as you learnt to balance, you learnt to take your first few pushes, develop your comfort in rolling, going slow, going fast, maybe learning to manipulate and move your board, followed by tic-tac, kickturn, carve, ollie, acid drop, drop in, whatever you want and however you like it.

Skateboarding has some key foundations to it that serve as building blocks. This happens in life through the milestones in your development that serve as foundations for your growth and further progress, like learning to communicate, move and coordinate your body. Despite having common things that we all learn as part of our journey through life and skateboarding, we all branch off on our own paths and have our own unique experience and development attached to it.

When you find your love for skateboarding, you'll find that it flows naturally. Progression is an essential and obvious part of the journey that is characterized by one's passion and enjoyment of it. What this has the power and potential to teach is that engaging in life from a perspective of appreciation, love and purpose allows us to flow from experience to experience with greater confidence, courage and commitment. As a grounding and very present-focussed activity to participate in, skateboarding empowers one to find purpose in their present and pay attention to who and what are really in the environment around them.

Skateboarding progresses naturally, in that it's not something that you can plan or set a timeframe on. There's an undefined amount of time for how long it may take you to learn to stand on board, learn to push, ollie and kickflip and so forth. Some people will have it figured out quickly, others may take longer. Some tricks may feel more comfortable or uncomfortable for you. You can commit to the experience and experiment by practising and reflecting on your skateboarding regularly but no one ever truly knows the details of when. It just happens when you focus on serving a dynamic purpose, which is a purpose that is flexible, ever-changing and evolving and you recognise the underlying intent of learning for the enjoyment and love of skateboarding. Purpose is not something that is fixed on achievement, a future moment that is set on a track or clearly defined by a timeframe, textbook or through the eyes of comparison with others.

There are times in your life when you will need to make decisions about your life and are asked questions like *"what do you want to do with your life?" "What will you do when you finish school, graduate from studies and come of age?"* Respectively speaking, while it's nice to have an ambition and an idea of what you want to do with your life, like a job or studying or running a business, this is a mindset focussed on being productive. Some people will have this plan figured out early on and others later on, which can feel stressful if there is pressure to have an answer or have something to show that they are growing up and being responsible.

Focusing only on the doing, as a representation of desire towards a projected future outcome and purpose creates the potential for judgment of self and others based on their answer to these questions. This also has its impacts on one's own appreciation of their own abilities and affects their relationships, self-esteem, self-worth and value of life. Everyone has their own timing in life, just like in skateboarding. Skateboarders communicating through the language of love, can understand the value of this timing and can usually show their acceptance for others and the different stages of their journeys because they can relate. They have been there before and they know what it's like.

To address this, an additional key question to focus on asking is, *"what do you want to be in your life?"* This ensures that the focus is on the present moment and the representation of purpose itself is flexible. There is the included opportunity to explore purpose in the context and realm of emotion and feeling the value of the situation.

What is most important is that we seek to serve a purpose rather than to have it so clearly defined with one straight purpose or mapped out on a set path. One's purpose can change many times throughout their lifetime and it isn't a static one-way path. While it is great to have aspirations and goals in mind, life isn't so much enriched by how many goals that one can achieve, but rather it's about the meaning behind them. Anything done with passion can illustrate this momentarily in the context of one's self-expression, while for skateboarding, this permeates holistically into life inside and outside of the activity itself.

When arriving at a skatepark or spot, is there a clear definition of how to skate it? Is there a set track in the bowl that you have to carve? Every place you'll ever skate is made differently and try as they may to replicate them, there'll always be differences in the physical and environment around them. Life is the same in this way. No one can ever tell you what your purpose is, you have to feel it for yourself. You will come to know what your purpose in life is through finding purpose in the everyday. Every expression of life has its own purpose, yet it isn't something that you need to constantly evaluate and make judgments of in comparison to others. Every individual has their own unique purpose to serve in the ways that they engage with the world within and all around them.

Focus on being your best, showing up in life in the greatest version of yourself rather than comparing yourself to others or trying to outdo them. The only real competitor you are up against is yourself. Strive to better yourself in ways that keep you in a state of love of what you are doing. Everyone has their own journey and their own experience of progress, which is the purpose of life itself.

Gather all the skills that you have learnt throughout your journey of Skateboarding and let them flow into all areas of your life. Each of us is here on this Earth to learn to experience and express love. Let Skateboarding be your ride through this.

Every path, every push.

Every person, every purpose.

Every purpose, every passion.

Skateboarders, Cause, Effect and Responsibility

You're standing on your skateboard and you bend your knees, press down on the tail of your board and what happens? Your board starts to rise vertically, as you jump up and in the same direction as you are rolling and simultaneously slide your front foot forward, allowing the friction of the grip tape to level out your board. You've left the ground, you've just done an ollie. You've practised this millions of times before right? Or you've the tail of your skateboard on the coping and put one foot on after the other, lean forward and drop into a transition? Or put one foot on the deck bolts and take a push to start rolling?

Anything that you do while you are on your skateboard is a prime example of cause and effect. Your movements with your skateboard send out energy which can be classified as the cause, while landing and rolling away can be classified as the effect. Through skateboarding's diversity and accessibility, people have different ways to interact and engage with their skateboard and the environment in which they find themselves in. Through changing the cause, skateboarders are able to express different effects in their skateboarding. These causes and effects are what make the process of skateboarding so enthralling and thrilling!

There is a wide range of variables that can influence the cause or the pre-determining factors of skateboard trick composition and this is something that

I'm sure you would have thought about in your own skating or when viewing skate photos and videos. There are environmental factors that influence the cause, such as the terrain and whether the ground or surface is cracked, smooth, rough or slippery, the pedestrian security guard and overall traffic situation and the times that these places can be skated. For the skater, there are personal variables such as approaching angle and speed, height and length of the object, skateboard ability, confidence and trick selection.

Considering all these different variables, there really is a lot going on when it comes to skateboarding. Much more than we realize, yet we are able to weave these factors altogether and one's ideas and movements merge with the environment.

While skateboarding itself happens quite quickly, the learning process will certainly show you that changes to your foot placement, body weight, approach and timing will bring you closer to or further away from your desired effect. I know the frustration in learning new tricks or skating new spots or having those days where skateboarding doesn't seem to be flowing. Think about the things that you can control instead of the things that you can't control and work on them. Change it up, simplify your approach, clear your mind. This is your responsibility, to change your input.

It certainly isn't your board's responsibility to flip slower or faster. Try changing your foot placement, flick your board with more control. It's not the spot's responsibility to change its surface so that you can roll there smoothly. Dealing with pedestrians and traffic, you're going to need to take responsibility for that by making wise decisions about when to go, perhaps having a friend to look for those perfect gaps in traffic for you to skate through.

As much as you'd like to make the security guards vanish and not care about where you're skating, it's not going to happen but if you're willing to skate at a spot with that potential, be responsible by being respectful, argue intelligently and in a non-threatening way, prepare to leave and try work out a more suitable time to return. There is a perfect time and place for everything, if not today, then maybe tomorrow or another time.

Although cause and effect are quite instantaneous in skateboarding, it's also worth remembering that we all need to take responsibility and become accountable for our own input into our causes. We are the ones in our own bodies and in our own minds and it's the power of choice and our own control that influences what happens on your skateboard.

Every cause sends energy into the world which is matched by the reception of a corresponding response from life itself. Everything that we think, say and do impacts us. Sometimes in life this can take a bit longer to show and skateboarding itself teaches lessons in cause and effect quite quickly, by the way the body and board move to leave the ground and gravity has its way of bringing us back to the ground.

Some thoughts and actions take longer for life to respond back with or are more subtle, like you know those days where you wake up feeling in a bad mood and everything and everyone around you seems to be an irritant or seemingly responsible for your day? Or like when you are sending out a certain vibe that everyone around you seems to be vibing off?

Typically when people are faced with situations that they don't find pleasant or enjoyable, they might complain about it. Complaining only brings focus on the negative emotions and experiences and doesn't pave the way forward. People complain about all sorts of things from small things like the service at the shops, the way they were spoken to, the food they eat, the habits they have formed and the behaviours of another individual, to big things like their job, spouse and coworkers.

What would you do if your ollies weren't high enough to get you onto or over that obstacle? Or you couldn't pump to keep up your speed? Or you couldn't get enough speed with one push to clear that gap or set of stairs? Would you keep complaining about it and doing the same thing?

Or would you change your approach?

Whatever it is, we have the power of choice. If there are effects that we don't like or are not satisfied with, we can take time to work on these things, knowing that we are responsible and what we input into these situations influences the effects and emotions related to those experiences. Through skateboarding as a life teacher of cause and effect, one is empowered to learn to balance out taking risks and responsibility for actions and choices as well as understand the interplays of sending and receiving energy in life.

Every thought, intention and action is met with a corresponding outcome and so we actually have so much influence into the very nature of our lives. Life is full of an abundance of choices and opportunities and there may be situations where people can become disconnected from their intentions and awareness of their present situation. They become drowned in the experience of their effects without much conscious attention on their causes. This can lead to two outcomes;

The first is based upon enjoying the seemingly pleasurable experiences with such intensity, to the degree that a dependency develops. This leads to a manifestation of addictive behaviours and reckless experiences that can follow, such as in the instances of excessive alcohol and drug abuse, sexual assault, driving offences and trouble with the law.

The second is based upon being so concerned about the effects of their thinking and actions and whether they are positive or negative. This creates experiences of extreme anxiety, isolation and worry.

Know the impact of the decisions that you make in life as your choices impact you and those around you. Recognise the level of control that you have and work with that. Engage in choices that make you and others feel empowered, rather than the ones that make everyone feel restricted, restrained or powerless. Be respectful with the power of choices, for this is a power that everyone deserves to have and remembers how to use.

Our choices can lead us to feel in situations at risk or reward. With conscious awareness of this, we are free from the fear of the loss and change of the desirable experiences and the worry that comes with repetition and recurrence of the undesirable experiences. When you are out skating, there is try or don't try, bail or bust, ride away or don't ride away. Some of these thoughts might cross your mind, but thoughts, like clouds in the sky, can pass and you'll find your way to do what you want to do, in perfect alignment with your own abilities, needs and placement within time and space itself.

Life is meant to be lived and enjoyed, just like how skateboarding is meant to be fun. There is no such thing as mistakes. Only experience and experiments. This shows up in skateboarding quite prevalently, so know that whatever the situation in life outside of skateboarding, your life can also change quickly through your intentions, thoughts and actions. The positive experiences can change and fade away just as the negative experiences can be turned around. What's significant to keep in mind is your presence and awareness. With what you experience, acknowledge it for what it is and change it if you desire to. Life is expansive and full of ripe opportunities to engage and connect with the world.

Skateboarding's paced in such a way that keeps us present and self-aware through every crucial moment on board. Every push, carve, kickturn and foot placement matters and has its place in the experience.
Everything in life and skateboarding has its place and purpose, without coincidence. Take this principle out of skateboarding and apply it to your life, knowing that ultimately, you are in control of the experience in your own body and mind.

Be conscious and aware yet accepting and compassionate for yourself and others in all situations and recognise how skateboarding and life can continue to progress and get better for everyone in this way.

Skateboarders and Sacred Space

What do you think of when you think of sacred space? A place of worship like a church or temple? A place that is designated specifically for its visitors to commune with the Divine? What does it mean for a place to be sacred? All spaces in the environment are sacred and go beyond the common perspective of a place being sacred only by its boundaries and the officials that designate it to be so.

Can the Divine only be experienced inside a particular place? Or is it that the Divine is experienced within, around and beyond the confines of a location? Like skateboarding, can you only skate in the skatepark or does skateboarding offer you freedom and exploration of a world beyond something that has been built for the specific purpose of skating?

Taking on this perspective allows us to become more aware of our surroundings and develop a greater appreciation for them. While it is a nice gesture and place of community, there are many similarities between practicing at a communal, purpose built environment for skateboarding and religious aspects of life. With what you develop and build, ideally are things that you learn, assimilate into your body, brain and lifestyle and take with you to serve the world and the streets, be it that lesson from the lecture or reading or that trick that you spent hours practicing.

Places are made sacred by their purpose and the people that participate. As you explore the world, you take your learnings and apply them to contexts outside of the place where you initially learnt them. Through life and the additional places you visit, you are turning every place into a sacred space by your presence and what you bring to the environment. There is no authority that deems whether one place is more sacred than another, however what this really means is that every place has the potential to be sacred. What makes this even more special in skateboarding is the way that tricks of skateboard photos and videos capture moments in time that make history and glorify the place and the participant. It shines a new light on the place, consecrating it with the magic of skateboarding.

All places in your environment can be considered sacred as you visit, explore and shine your light on board and off board. All places store the energy of the activities that take place within them and all places have contextual factors that apply to them which enable its visitors to effectively and respectfully participate in the activities of that space. These include factors such as being mindful of those around them, the cleanliness and rubbish, noise levels and looking out for one another. While these are unwritten and generally understood by everyone, they are factors that generally apply everywhere you go.

As skateboarding can be any place, any time, consider all spots that you visit as sacred. Skateboarders can sometimes be perceived as intimidating to the misinformed outsider. Consider what you can do to your vibe to shine a positive light on the environments you visit. What can you and your friends do to show that you are making the place sacred?

Take care of the places that you visit and infuse them with your love and presence. Whether you are at a skatepark or skating in the streets, leave behind no rubbish, be mindful of the volume of your voices, any swearing or explicit language, any deliberate damage to property. There's a difference between skating an obstacle or making an obstacle out of something in the streets and deliberately climbing on, taking apart and breaking something for attention and approval of peers.

What if you were consecrating and blessing every place you set foot on? Skateboarding's accessibility gives purpose to and brings life to a range of environments, especially if those places are overlooked, perhaps neglected environments that are not frequented by many.

Whether you are seeking to understand more about life or skateboarding, there are many ways to pray and play, worship and practise. Some may prefer a purpose built environment, while others may prefer to develop through their own interactions and exploration of the world. Regardless of what one has preference for, all locations can become the altar or dedicated and devoted space to express and explore one's inner and outer world.

Who would've ever thought that skateboarding had the power to consecrate environments and make them a pilgrimage site for other skateboarders far and wide? Any place, any time, Skateboarding is an act of self-cultivation, co-ordinating body, mind and spirit and connection to your board and the world around.

The world is your skatepark just as the world is your sacred site.

Keep an open mind and think outside the box.

Skate to create!

Skateboarders and Compassion

What does it mean to be compassionate? To love and be loved? To understand and welcome each and all? To be kind to one's self and to others? To discover the possibilities of being accepting and accepted?

Skateboarding's accessibility means that it is available to anyone and everyone, regardless of the usual factors that people base their friendships on, such as age, gender, sexual preference, social status, employment, culture, recreational preferences outside of Skateboarding and so on. Skateboarding has an appeal that reaches out to many people from all different walks of life.

Idealistically, compassion is taught about in educational institutes and religions, the only way to verify the truth of these teachings is through application. I think that Skateboarding has its way of teaching this in a very clear and concise way. Skateboarding teaches these lessons of understanding and ac-ceptance very effectively through the very nature of the people that are ex-perienced, both the desired and undesired.

The desirable people in your range of experiences consist of the people that you want around, such as your fellow skateboarders, your friends. It's easy to accept and understand your friends through your shared experiences and being able to relate to some elements of the journey to learn and progress in skateboarding.

Building bonds with the people that you hang around and skate with occurs because you can relate to one another, you empathise and you celebrate each others' achievements. Whether you are skating the same spot, different spots, trying the same or different tricks, playing a game of S.K.A.T.E, shooting a photo or video, a win for one is a win for all.

The experience you seek is different, but the feeling and vibe behind it is all so similar. Skateboarding is an activity that facilitates the release of feel-good brain chemicals, so it's only natural to feel on a high and want to share it with others that are also participating in the environment around you.

The undesirable people that you experience in skateboarding are true tests of what you learn about in your understanding and the application of acceptance and compassion during moments of confrontation. These people might range from the nosy neighbours, heroic bystander, angry shopkeeper, security guard or police officer that shows up to spoil your fun, say if you're out skating in a place that may not be an 'approved' place to play.

When you get excited about skating at a spot in the streets, maybe one that hasn't skated before, or one that you have some good trick ideas for, your feel-good brain chemicals are already starting to flow. You start trying a few, maybe flicking your board around, warming up and getting a feel for the spot and then someone shows up to try to put an end to it.

What do you do when you are faced with a high and a potential low? It's probably going to feel like a bit of an emotional rollercoaster going from the high to low, especially if you are faced with someone else's anger and authority. There are probably going to be times where you might be ill-treated because of what you appear to be doing, that is, skating in a place that someone thinks you shouldn't be. What do you do in these situations? What can you do to hold it all together in these times? What does the best version of you look like in these moments?

Do you ride the tidal wave of emotion and return the anger, project your frustration or respond in an intimidating way? What are the consequences and how do these experiences leave you feeling afterwards?

Consider the buildup of tension and the kind of emotion that you are expressing. They might not be fellow skateboarders, but they are your fellow human beings!

The mark of victory in these circumstances is not over who wins and who gets their way, but rather who is able to maintain their emotional composure. The moment someone else frustrates you is the moment that you give your power away because you are allowing the emotion of the experience to consume and control you. In order to maintain your high vibration of compassion, which then contributes to experiences of continued joy and elation afterwards, there are several factors that you can consider understanding, to keep you vibing high and rolling on afterwards in a better frame of mind.

Understand where they are coming from. A security guard or a police officer might be simply doing their job if you're there during their official duty. A member of the public might be trying to express their concerns. Recognise that their frustration is a reflection of their own inner struggle that they are working through too. Perhaps they are used to being met with such hostility in their own emotional responses to different situations. Empathise with them and acknowledge their concerns, discuss intelligently, resist the temptation to swear or unleash verbal abuse at them for spoiling your fun. Wait for things to cool off and diffuse the situation. Wait and try to find a more accept-able time to return if you need to. Celebrate the fact that perhaps you tried or experienced something new with your skating. Even if you didn't land your trick in mind, perhaps it's a stepping stone to your building confidence for another time or another place.

It's the thrill of all these alignments that adds to the fulfilment and the joys of skateboarding. Rising above and beyond the often limited perceptions of what others expect within the confines of an environment and finding your own way to navigate and negotiate through the world, physically, emotionally, mentally and spiritually.

Life as a skateboarder combines on board and off board experiences that can enrich one's ability to understand and relate to people within and outside of skateboarding itself. Love prevails above all other emotions and if you roll around with intentions of acceptance, compassion, kindness and understanding, it shows up as your vibration.

The way that you experience others shifts and the way that people respond to you changes. Be a better person and live and lead life with an open-mind and an open-heart. As much as others may appear to get in the way, they can never truly stop or prevent you from skateboarding.

Let your love of skateboarding be what carries you through to the next spot, the next day and the next person.

Skateboarding as Prayer and Meditation

Skateboarding has been a big part of my life for over 20 years. I've always loved all things skateboarding, just finding ways to be involved and keep the fire burning. One of the big lessons that I've learnt through skateboarding is that as the years go by, your expression or interests can change, you might find a different way to skate or enjoy skating differently to when you first started out, yet your passion and enjoyment for it doesn't.

I know that commonly, prayers are thought of as an element of connecting with the Divine, commonly found in a religious kind of way. Prayer could also be defined as a powerful way to be in the present in the moment and a way of relating to the Divine, ourselves and others.

Skateboarding can do that and more! The Divine is a state of being that resides within and all around you, you that is creative, compassionate and loving. Prayer brings people together. Skateboarding brings people together. Those that pray together stay together. Those that play together stay together. You open each other up, you bond, you communicate, you raise the energy.

You find inspiration in your inner and outer world. You set out to learn something new or master it in your own way, you find a way to express this and you celebrate your successes, as do others. You connect with history and become a part of paving and co-creating history. You draw on your inspiration from those who came before you and you become inspiration for those after you. The skateboard experience is such a visual journey and so the representation of it found in artifacts such as photos and videos play such an important role in helping to connect skateboarders across time and space.

I feel like this is where one connects with the real essence of skateboarding. When they pay their respects to the generations past, present and future, experience and enjoy the process of learning, expressing and sharing, in the spirit of non-competitive, non-judgmental kinds of ways. Your Heart and Soul goes into skateboarding when it is done with love and respect and there's something for everyone. As you roll further along on this path, skateboarding opens you up to other people and other interests, yet the mindset that you can experience from it stays with you for life.

This then leads us into the meditative aspects of skateboarding, which exists during the times when you become so focussed that you enter a transcended state of being. You go beyond your limitations, doubts and fears. You might accomplish something that you look at differently when you are off your Skateboard. You know that feeling of looking at a spot or reviewing a photo or footage after you've skated it, thinking like, *"wow, how did that actually happen?"*

I know that a lot of skateboarders can relate to the feeling and process of learning and trying a trick and then being astounded by the results afterwards. The reward isn't just in the result, but also in the emotional connection and state of being that comes from it.

Typically, there are a lot of questions and a lot of factors to consider when skateboarding. For instance:
- *What do your feet need to do?*
- *How should you position your body and body weight?*
- *What's happening in your surroundings?*
- *Are there other Skaters to look out for?*
- *What speed do I need to approach at?*
- *Are there any cracks? Are there oncoming pedestrians or traffic?*

- *Is there someone at the spot that will try to prevent you from Skating?*
- *What angle do you need to ride up to the obstacle at?*
- *What are your options if you need to jump off?*
- *Is the tripod, person filming or shooting set up and ready?*
- *When I eject my board, are they safe?*
- *Do I have a person Board-saving in case my Board goes onto the road or into the direction of other people?*
- *Is there rain or wind affecting my ability to skate this spot?*

When reflecting on this, there are so many questions that would be asked, so many factors that could create a lot of mental chatter. Many might think that the meditative aspect of skateboarding involves only blocking out the mental thoughts that emerge. What is really necessary to enhance one's mental clarity and focus is understanding what to concentrate on, physically, mentally and emotionally. Rather than ignoring the questions, answer them with clarity for peace of mind, assertiveness so that it becomes your mantra and control what is within your control.

Skateboarders require this kind of dedicated and directed attention while being able to answer these questions, let go of the distractions and be very present and in the moment. It can be easy to fixate on some of these questions while Skateboarding and feel stuck or think that certain feats are not possible. However with practice, one reaps confidence and with confidence, there is intention and desire. It's the meditation and trance-like experience of Skateboarding that gets us beyond all of the questions.

You might start with these factors and questions in mind when you get to your spot and you start warming up for your trick. You might start doing a few practice moves or start flicking your board. You might try and visualize what to do. You might start rolling around, finding that line, trying and committing to landing and roll if you're feeling it, if it feels good. You go above, below and through. You carve, kick turn, balance, grind, slide. You flip, catch, land. You roll away. The energy is high. You celebrate yourself. Your friends cheer you on. You replay the footage and see if it came out alright. You watch it again and again. You're on a high from your victory.

I know that there is a transformation of consciousness that takes place on a Skateboard. To the uninitiated and outside onlookers, it might look like a wheeled, wooden toy. It might look like another *"sport"* choice. It might look like a dangerous, disruptive or juvenile activity that damages urban environments.

To the initiated, they are alchemists. They transform lead to gold. They transform their own physical, mental, emotional and spiritual limits. The alchemist tests their body, mind and spirit. They learn to let go, they learn to commit and trust themselves and their board. They experience what it feels like to roll away and to keep rolling along.

I know that these kinds of experiences evoke a sense of feeling high. They release a combination of feel-good brain chemicals such as Dopamine, Oxytocin, Serotonin and Endorphins, which are great at leaving you feeling happy, connecting with others, sleeping better, releasing anxiety, stress and rolling into older age! While medical research stipulates that the Pineal Gland calcifies in older age, leading to disrupted hormones, affecting things like sleep, moods and energy levels, amongst other things, research has also shown that meditative experiences contribute to healthy stimulation of the Pineal Gland.

I know that skateboarders know and crave these feelings. It keeps them youthful and I know that many skateboarders see the world differently after these deep and meaningful experiences. A skateboarder's interaction and exploration of the world is similar to that of a Yogi. There are parallels between the ways they both connect and seek presence in their bodies. The level of attention and focus to push themselves and open themselves up beyond limitations of the body, mind and spirit.

Skateboarding builds character. It connects one with their Soul. Though it can be seen as fast paced and noisy by some, it's meditation in movement. Skateboarders are pushed to be in their altered state quite quickly. This is how skateboarding is enjoyed best — focussed and fun.

I recognize this when I see people skating and they're having fun. They're focussed and they're enjoying it because it's working for them and they're focussed on things that uplift them. The days that it's not working, the days that boards get thrown around, deliberately broken, they're the days with distractions; interferences getting in the way of one's ability to concentrate.

Skateboarding's message is simple.

Have fun. Find joy through play. Explore creativity through self-expression. Bond with others through sharing love. Focus on what you want rather than what you don't want. Become immersed in your inner and outer world and share the feelings and high vibes around with loved ones. This is the essence of skateboarding!

Skateboarding and Spiritual Maintenance

What is the first thing that comes to mind when thinking about maintenance of your skateboard? What about the maintenance of your spirit?

Living in a world that is made up of matter, it is safe to say that we live in a world that is full of energy. There are energetic phenomena which we know exist, even if we can't typically see or touch it in a physical way, such as electricity and oxygen. The energy that we will be focussing on in this chapter is based on the concept of life-force energy, also known as Chi, Ki or Prana.

Life-Force Energy flows through every living being and consists of several layers of bio-electrical energy that science acknowledges and is able to measure with electromagnetic resonance technology or Kirlian Photography. This energy flows through our bodies through a network of pathways, called meridians. It is important to keep this energy flowing and circulating throughout the body for optimum physical, mental, emotional and spiritual health.

Our energy flow is literally what allows us to feel vibrant and full of vitality or drained, exhausted and fatigued and can be influenced by a range of different factors including thoughts, emotions, experiences, actions, interactions and the foods, drinks and substances that we ingest.

Your Life-Force Energy can be likened to your skateboard bearings that keep your wheels turning. If you have clean and well-lubricated bearings, your wheels will spin faster. You'll know when your bearings are in need of a service when your wheels start making clunky noises, spin slower or stop spinning altogether. Ideally, you want to avoid popping any bearings and having your wheel come off mid-session right?

When we have an understanding of Life-Force Energy, the things that affect it and how to maintain it, it will be similar to understanding the maintenance needs of skateboard bearings. You might feel like cleaning, degreasing and oiling your bearings with some speed cream or other forms of lubrication might not be that necessary, as you can easily purchase a new set of bearings when they feel worn out. You might be able to manage with bearings that wear out and just replace them individually. These are examples of two ways to handle this in a short-term and long-term sense; purchasing new ones and replacing them every time they stop spinning or learning the skills to maintain and manage your bearings, empowering you to take control.

The same can be said about our Life-Force Energy. There are methods of replenishing our energetic needs through short-term and long-term means. Short-term means might involve the use of substances such as alcohol, cigarettes and other stimulants, while long-term means might involve breathwork, energy healing modalities, emotional release, meditation and other forms of self-healing to manage energy flow for the purpose of feeling relaxed, rejuvenated and revitalised.

Looking at both the maintenance of skateboard bearings and Life-Force Energy, short-term means usually involve some form of expenditure, while long-term means usually involve the learning of a skill to manage your own energy flow.

While there is no right or wrong way to manage your skateboard bearings or your life-force energy, there is an impact on the overall performance of your skateboard wheels and personal energy flow. Should you decide to discover more about the processes of maintenance, you'll be learning skills, furthering your understanding and application of skills on a very personal and powerful level. In a fast-paced world where information and resources are readily available at our fingertips, we can choose to feed either decision. These aren't common conversations that you'll have with others, yet learning to maintain and restore your bearings and or your own Life-Force Energy are skills that can be acquired with patience and dedication and can deepen your passion and understanding of skateboarding and life.

Naturally as you skate with bearings in your wheels, they are going to show some signs of wear. The outer bearing casings can accumulate dirt, dust, grime and other things in them that can slow down the speed of rotation of the bearings and wheels. These obstructions are like baggage that can get in between the wheel, bearing and axle, where the wheel spins. To clean these casings is quick, low-level maintenance — you could wipe them down with a rag. Leaving your bearing casings and letting these things accumulate end up slowing you down.

With your Life-Force Energy, interactions with the world outside of you form into energetic attachments with the different people, places and things that you interact with, that can slow down your flow. Clairvoyantly, these show up as cords or hooks that extend outward from an individual and in a more practical-grounded sense, these are characterised in the form of unhealthy attachments and dependencies on people, places and things outside of you and feeling depleted, drained or exhausted after day to day interactions.

There are many different things that can help you to engage in the low-level maintenance of your Life-Force Energy. Here are some of the things that work for me that I also teach to my Students. They work wonderfully, so you might like to give these some consideration:
- Take moments during your day to become aware of your breath. Practise inhaling, deep breaths into the belly for a count of 5 and exhaling, deep breaths out for a count of 5. Set the intention to inhale desirable, positive emotions, while releasing anything you wish to clear with every exhale that no longer serves you.
- Cord cutting by using your hands to make sweeping motions at the level of your Sternum (Solar Plexus). Sweep as if you're making a cutting motion,

once with your left hand, once with your right hand and once more with both hands at the same time.
- At the end of each day, visualizing yourself standing under a Silver Waterfall that cleanses you and your body of all the energy and emotions that don't belong to you or you no longer need.
- Like cleaning the cases of your skateboard bearings, low-level maintenance methods are a quick way to check in with yourself and how you're rolling (energetically and emotionally). At first, these might seem like unusual or foreign practises to engage with, however with practice, you'll start to develop more awareness and sensitivity to the ways that energy and emotions can affect you. Leaving these excess energies to accumulate slows down the flow of your Life-Force Energy, in a similar way to letting excess grime, dirt and other things build up and restrict the rotation of your skateboard wheels.

This brings us into the concept of shielding. While it is up to individual preference, some skaters like to take the shields off their bearings for several reasons including appearance, aesthetics, sound and benefits to speed. The only drawback being that they are open and exposed to more elements that can build up and slow them down. Some might choose to pop the shields off their bearings when skating a park, for maximum speed in a clean, wheel-friendly environment, while keeping them on when skating in the street or in a pool, where there might be more dust, dirt and grime. Skaters can decide on this for themselves and apply their preferences depending on their situation. It is through these options that skaters can be more conscious and mindful of where they are rolling and how their wheels are impacted.

Shielding your energy, is something that a lot of older generation spiritual teachers may advocate for, which usually involves things such as carrying specific crystals, using a certain essential oil or herb, visualising one to multiple bubbles or capsules of colour and light around you, pulling your energy back into yourself and avoiding people, places, things and situations that may drain your energy. Shielding your energy is a personal preference similar to deciding whether or not to skate with shields on your bearings or to skate with bearings shieldless.

Sure your energy might feel more reserved and essentially yours if you are avoiding everyone and everything and isolating yourself, but how will that encourage you to connect with others, serve the community and share your gifts and talents with the world? If you are fearful of being vulnerable and close yourself off, you also run the risk of compromising friendships, relationships. It's the same door in and the same door out. Living in constant fear of expending your energy or picking up on others' energy and emotions can make you paranoid and withdrawn.

In the context of your Life-Force Energy, the gift of sensitivity is sensitivity. It's through the availability of the preferences to shield or not to shield, that one can develop their awareness and understanding of how different energies can affect them. As you open yourself up to others, you open up to yourself too. Your decision to shield your energy might depend on the context and environment that you are in. For instance, you might like to shield yourself more in a very crowded environment that can leave you feeling exhausted and stressed, while with close friends or family, you might like to ease off on the shielding so that you can be more emotionally available and vulnerable to them.

You can allow yourself to adapt to your situation, for you would still want to be able to benefit from being around others, while still being able to flourish emotionally and energetically. It's personal preference to shield or not to shield your bearings or energy and they are decisions that can support the development of your own inner wisdom on and off your skateboard.

Every once in a while, you might feel the need to do a replacement or service of your bearings and carry out a degreasing, cleaning and lubricating ritual. You'll know when it's time, when your bearings aren't rolling as smoothly or are making noises that you didn't hear before. The need for deeper spiritual maintenance can be characterized by factors such as recurring or unresolved behaviours, feelings of being stuck or lost in life, experiencing fear and trauma, attracting similar experiences, people and relationships into your life and unprocessed, buried emotions. These things can impact upon your everyday life, personal and professional relationships and your overall health and wellbeing.

The low-level maintenance of your skateboard bearings or your spiritual-self focusses on what's on the surface, the more noticeable everyday kind of factors and is carried out more frequently. The higher-level maintenance goes deeper into layers upon layers of energy and might only undertaken once or twice a year and can delve into areas such as reprogramming beliefs, transforming negative patterns, resolving cellular memories from current or past lifetimes, clearing lodgements in your energy field, accessing your Soul's records (Akashic Records) to learn more about your gifts, talents and purpose.These are probably topics for another discussion, however raising your awareness of these can encourage you to explore if you so wish.

When you have serviced your bearings it feels like your bearings are brand new at their optimum performance. The same goes for your spiritual maintenance. When you explore and experience your spiritual maintenance in this capacity, you'll feel like parts of you are reborn again. You may experience shifts in your consciousness which can help you to feel a renewed sense of appreciation, confidence and clarity about your life and the world that you live in.

The maintenance of your bearings and your spirit are both delicate, dedications to yourself and the vehicles that you are traveling in to traverse through skateboarding and life. When considering the concept of maintenance, it raises the question of how far you are willing to go within in order to take care of, clean, nurture and restore the very parts of you and your life that you love.

Maintenance conveys the idea of seeking continual improvement and care for you and your equipment and to empower you to deliver your best in any given situation. Everyone can access the tools to maintain their skateboard bearings and their spiritual selves by reaching out, making connections, asking questions and doing their research. There is no rule in skateboarding or in life about what to do, how to do it, or even whether one should or shouldn't when it comes to maintenance. It is entirely up to you, the skater and the seeker.

Skateboarding: Empowerment, Enrichment & Enlightenment

What is enlightenment and how does one reach this state? Is it considered a state of being Saint-like or is it only attainable by the holy, devout followers of a specific path? Which spiritual path is the best and which one is correct? Which path is going to bring peace when so many preach different things?

Typically religions and cults are made up of similar organisational structures consisting of a main driving force, purpose or principle, perhaps a deity or divinity, leaders and facilitators and lastly, followers or practitioners. The leader is the one who is the facilitator that manages exchange of knowledge and it is up to the practitioner to practise and apply what they have learnt to their lives. Some of these paths, not all, have strict rules to follow and its facilitators exercise a degree of control over its practitioners through conveying fear. While living by specific rules as part of a religious path may be seen as a form of building discipline and foundation values, it can also drive followers in the direction of suppressing their own needs, embarking on blind faith and dedication without questioning what they are doing and why.

What can occur in some of these organizational structures is that followers turn their power over to facilitators and can become dependent on them for their own spiritual nourishment. The facilitators, leaders and figure-heads of some of these groups get put onto a pedestal and they become deified in their own sense because of their perceived greater connection and communication with the Divine. When this happens, people in these organizations forget that these leaders are living through the Human Experience too — the full spectrum of all human emotions, desires and needs. The hierarchy model tends to create separation between all people and the different levels of power and healthy expressions of their humanity.

In the worst case scenarios, people in these higher positions of hierarchy in an organised religion or cult, abuse this power through harsh judgements and punishments, emotional manipulation and expressing distortions of their Human needs and emotions which people tend to turn a blind-eye to. It is important to remember that everyone is a Spiritual Being living a Human Experience and because of this, we all have an equal opportunity to connect with the Divine. There is no need to turn your power over to someone else because of their experiences, for you are the one living in your own body and mind. Your experience will be truly unique to you. Everyone has their own pathway to connect with the divine while also having the permission to be human and expressive in healthy ways.

While a structured or organized spiritual path like a religion, can be a helpful place to begin for some to be introduced to and build the foundations of a spiritual path, it could also be likened to the process of learning skateboard tricks. Some might start out with skateboard coaching or lessons to learn some basic techniques and as progression takes place, is there a limit or defined prescription of techniques and tricks that one has to learn? Can the unlimited potential of creativity in skateboarding be contained within the instruction of another, or through the context of a video, magazine, book or website?

The experience and nature of divinity like skateboarding is also unlimited. It can't be contained within the walls of a building or place of worship, serving as a reminder that a Spiritual path is not a one-size fits all experience and cannot be taught through one organisation or a set of lifestyle rules alone.

What makes skateboarding so enriching, empowering and enlightening is that it has no gurus, figureheads or leaders. It isn't organised in a hierarchy and inspires its participants to look within. Yes, there are people that you can look up to and be inspired by, but there is no one giving instructions on which principles to apply to your life. *"Take what you will from skateboarding and skateboarders and make it your own"* is one of the key messages found in skateboarding. Because of the absence from organisation and hierarchy, skateboarders of all ages and backgrounds can relate to each other and learn to appreciate the shared environment. It doesn't matter what your skill level is, whether you are a beginner or veteran, sponsored or unsponsored, professional or skating for fun, skateboarding welcomes everyone to have a choice and a voice.

Reflecting on my experiences of organized religion, I always felt disconnected from the nature of the hierarchy, in that I found it difficult to relate to the teacher and teachings, to make understanding of them and express myself in meaningful ways. When I began skateboarding, I discovered more significant and relatable role-models and life lessons than any congregation or community could share. It was the recognition of the spiritual and the human qualities of the skateboarders around me that really helped to mould my understanding of the world within and all around.

Stars of the skateboard world are immortalized in their glory through the abundance of photos and videos found in print and digital formats. In the past, Skaters could only see their favourite skaters in monthly magazines and annual video parts on VHS and DVD. Only skaters who were equipped with cameras and video cameras could participate in documenting their skating. Skateboarding had barriers, which has now all changed with the onset of the Internet and digital age.

The era of the internet has lowered these barriers. The Internet has made Skateboarding open and available to everyone. Skateboarders are united around the world through the Internet, skateboard companies and their representatives have more interaction with their audiences. Skaters can easily seek out, create and publish their own content from the use of a phone. The bonds and connection between Skateboarders has become even greater. Improved communication has enabled more opportunities for Skaters to connect from around the world and relate to different elements of the Skateboarder's journey, which is such an incredible facet of Skateboarding to experience and explore.

Skateboarding has no leaders, it has no one telling you how or where to skate. It's just you and your board. You can certainly be inspired by other skateboarders and learn from them, maybe even be mentored by some of them, but the experience is going to be very individualized for you as you are the only one living in your body, mind and spirit.

No one else is going to progress you on your path for you. Skateboarding teaches its participants to embark on self-discovery. For instance, you might seek out some pointers or trick tip tutorials which can give you some guidance and show you things like foot positioning and board movements, but for you to be able to learn and apply it, you'll need to try it for yourself. Practice, practice, practice!

Skateboarding's DIY approach pushes skaters to find and pave their own path. It's one for all and all for one. The nature of learning Skateboarding through observation, experiment and experience instills qualities of resilience and dedicated intention, which optimizes qualities of independence and self-efficacy in Skateboarders. This serves as fuel for Skateboarders and their incredible ability to create something from nothing. For generations and generations, Skateboarders seek out the skateable and if there isn't anything there, they'll create their own spots and build their own obstacles.

Through thinking about these qualities of Skateboarding, there is great capacity for one to experience immense spiritual growth and transformation. In truth, everyone has the equal opportunity to become enlightened in Skateboarding and life. Everyone has the ability to take what they learn and apply it. Through application, one is able to verify whether or not it has truth, significance and relevance through their own experiences.

For one to have a truly deep and meaningful spiritual path, one has to be able to ask questions, live out their experiences and relationship with the Divine and understand how they influence their own lives and are co-creators with the Divine, not simply subservient beings that turn over their power and will to others. Skateboarding, as a lifestyle, art form and experience offers these experiences in a very grounded and practical manner. Skateboarding reminds us that divinity exists and expresses itself from within each and all of us and the experiences are not just reserved for those in power.

Afterword by Nathan

The satisfaction and delight in writing The Endless Wave can be compared to the feeling of having a great day Skating where everything flowed, something new was learnt or a trick was filmed. The Endless Wave was a truly remarkable process and something that I never imagined doing as a skateboarder and an author.

From the initial moments of its inception all the way through to the end of writing, the words poured out every writing session without any writer's block. I had taken a break from writing for quite some time and I was looking to begin a new project once I had more clarity on the direction, intention and purpose behind it. I could liken this experience to the times when I haven't skated for a period of time due to injuries, family, school, work or other circumstances and the return to skateboarding is like the spark of an explosion of expression for skateboarding.

When I wrote my sections for this book, I was recovering from a second knee surgery and had plenty of time to reflect on skateboarding and its meaning in my life. The time that I spent off board helped me to remain connected with skateboarding in another way and was a pathway to discover what it truly meant to be a skateboarder. The elements of skateboarding analyzed in Endless Wave felt like great metaphors for exploring different elements of life, death and beyond.

Skateboarding is such a powerful medium for exploring one's self and the world. The potential for skateboarding in this capacity is far greater than what we realize. The Endless Wave isn't an instructional book or one that preaches spirituality and it isn't a book telling you how to live or how to skate. Rather it's about sharing some of the perspectives that form a way to understand the world and presenting you with the opportunity to take away what you will, form your own understanding and apply it to your life in your own way. My intention is that The Endless Wave inspires your first push inwards on that journey of self-actualization.

This is my first time co-authoring a publication with anyone and it turned out to be a very thought provoking and fulfilling process. Through this experience, we were able to approach discussions from different perspectives and provide insights into what we might see and what we might not see, behind the scenes in both skateboarding and life, death and beyond.

In opening myself up to authentically expressing the similarities between spirituality and skateboarding, I have been able to step into a position of greater self-acceptance appreciation and understanding of what it means to be a spiritual being having a skateboarding experience, not just a skateboarder having a spiritual experience.

If you enjoyed reading this book or have any questions on concepts that you would like to ask any questions about, please send me an email at *ooksvision@gmail.com*

For more information about the work and services that I have on offer, please visit my website at *www.nathanstar.com* or find me on Instagram *@nathanstarho*

Millions of articles, books, videos, podcasts and pieces of art are dedicated to the ideas surrounding death and dying. But I'd wager a large fortune that very few of them give a perspective of death and dying through the lens of a skateboarder.

This book aims to do just that — or at least start a conversation or two.

PUBLISHED BY
TimeForMyStory.com

www.ingramcontent.com/pod-product-compliance
Lightning Source LLC
Chambersburg PA
CBHW051547010526
44118CB00022B/2609